CALL ME

Anne

CALL ME
Anne

ANNE HECHE

VIVA
EDITIONS

Published in the United States by Viva Editions, an imprint of Start Midnight, LLC, 221 River Street, Ninth Floor, Hoboken, New Jersey 07030.

Printed in the United States
Cover design: Jennifer Do
Cover photo: Maiwenn Raoult
Author make-up: Gregory Arlt
Author hair: Jon Lieckfelt
Text design: Frank Wiedemann

First Edition.
10 9 8 7 6 5 4 3 2 1

Trade paper ISBN: 978-1-62778-331-6
E-book ISBN: 978-1-62778-544-0

*This book is dedicated to Homer Heche,
Atlas Heche Tupper, and Heather Duffy—
the proof that love is real.*

I believe in life everlasting. I believe it is ours to choose. For all the rest of my time on this earth, I choose to live to the fullest of my potential. I wake each day to another adventure and seek the wisdom it offers. That is the truth of me. The joy I feel in that commitment has provided me with purpose, love, meaning, and excitement. This is what I share.

This is what I care about.

TABLE OF CONTENTS

How To Use This Book

No one chooses the circumstances they are born into. I was born into a family culture of abuse. It took years to come to terms with that, and honestly, it's a lifetime's work that will always be ongoing. This book is meant to give you a glimpse into that lifetime. It's a guidebook to some of the lessons I've learned over time and contains suggestions about how to put those lessons into practice in your own life. Every phase of life has had lessons for me, and my hope is that what I've learned might help ease the way for other people.

Even those fortunate enough not to be born into difficult situations experience trauma through their time on this earth. But in learning from your life, you don't have to reinvent the wheel. There are situations that you can't control; all you can control is how you react to them.

The lessons I share here come from my own life. Experience is the best teacher, and everyone learns from their own mistakes—but you can also learn from mine. Each chapter in this book is divided into three parts: a lesson, a practice, and a challenge.

The lessons are stories from my life. The practices are behaviors I learned along the way, which I hope will be inspiring for you and help shape the way you think about your own reactions and responses. The challenges are exercises, often creative, to help you process your own life and experiences and to help you think of ways to amplify the joy in your life.

This book is meant to be fun! While the practice of joy as I try to live it is a serious philosophy, it is also a process of finding happiness and laughter in your life and making these gifts a more central part of your days. I hope you will find the challenges interesting, thought-provoking, and fun as you bring a new lens to bear on your own experiences.

Start With The Heart

FLIPPING THE DIME:
A WARRIOR'S CHALLENGE

There is no proof that your voice matters in this world. There's no confirmation that what you're doing is right or what you think matters. In fact, *mattering* is the challenge. How we know we matter is by the way we make people feel in our presence.

If you were raised in an environment similar to mine, mattering was not at the top of the list of priorities. With my parents, when it came to the children, we were the fault line that allowed them to escape responsibility for the very fact that they'd had us.

Great. Someone to blame. It seemed to work so well, I learned to want someone to blame—other than myself. *I want that. I want the luxury to give up responsibility for my own actions, too* . . . But that would have been too easy, and I have never done things the easy way.

Why do I have to answer to myself? From before I can remember, I took responsibility for others. For everybody. For anybody. It's still a habit of mine I find hard to break. If you're fucked up or an underdog, I love you. I'll do anything for you! I could be having dinner with the most famous person on the planet, but I'll probably end up knowing more about the waitress by the end of the night.

My mother's favorite (and only) story about me as a girl is that I spent so much time cleaning toilets at home that when I was lucky enough to be in a restaurant, I'd clean the sinks in the bathroom as perfectly as I did at home. I did it so that the next customer would get the full experience of the restaurant. "She cleans so well at home," my mother would brag, "she does it in public!"

I always did everything I was asked to do, to the best of my ability. In my childhood, it meant my survival.

One of the hardest things to put into practice is that who you are is not defined by the hand you were dealt. And the most complicated relationship between doubt and trust that you will be called to answer is the question of who you are. The stories I share here are the ones I've asked my higher power to illuminate for me that will hopefully allow the opening to freedom and risk within yourself, to become wholly who you are, if that's what you want. I'm only on the path, guided by honesty and belief, that if I *listen*, I will be rewarded with love.

And it is so. Everywhere I go, everywhere I seek, I am greeted with angels of goodness. I am greeted with joy because I give it and I am always looking for it—it's my hope that you will, too. I am committed to delving deeper into myself so that I may continue to engage in life's offering, that I may have more stories to tell. More acceptance to behold. More compassion to give.

More love.

Love is confusing. It means something different to everyone. No one knows another's definition. We're forced to wonder when we encounter another whether they agree with us. Yet, have we even decided for ourselves? What are *our* guiding principles? How do we act upon them? Are we interested in *theirs*? Do they know *ours*? Have we shared? Do others care about what I feel? What does love mean to me? Are they interested in whether or not I care about what love means to them?

Are we *different*? Are we the *same*? Have we bothered to *ask*? Does love have a meaning to us? To others? Is love a foundation we seek? Is love the most important question to ask ourselves, and is love's meaning the one and only answer we're seeking? It may not be for everyone, but it has been for me. What's meaningful to you?

I've come to believe we have everything we need to make a life of joy, if only we embrace it. Live in loving kindness. Seems like a simple practice, yet how many have agreed to abide in misery or discontent? How many have gone along to get along at the expense of their own happiness?

I seek totality, unity, and harmony. I do not have all the answers, but I have found some through years of working to overcome the struggles I was born into. I am guided by both my higher power and by the importance of bringing more love and kindness into the world. I serve the wisdom that I have learned, what I have sought, and what I believe to be true. Love is all, and consciousness is the one and only guiding light. I am not for those who believe in a redemption society; no person is "less than" in my religion. I am for all those present, conscious, and loving beings who seek a world of unity and peace that demands love's totality: all for one. We must look out for ourselves and one another. We must make choices that are guided by truth, love, and kindness.

Love is a commitment to yourself. Love is the key that triggers the consciousness to decide just what it is we are here to accomplish. Loving consciousness is the agreement that empowers our bodies to activate the interaction with the universe that allows us to see another with clarity, nonjudgment, and compassion. We can join together in the greatest gift life offers: the activation of love and kindness to each other that is a heaven on earth.

My philosophy is simple. It's been crafted through decades of study. Put simply, I try to make sense out of nonsense. Life's challenges offer opportunities to sift through your own experiences and identify what makes sense to you and what you can take forward with you to overcome future challenges. The realization that I've come to is that the answers that are delivered in the simplest of ways are *the* answers.

The key is this statement: "I choose love."

Love is the first step on the pathway to total integration with your own humanity. Love is also the key to joy and happiness and to a better a world for future generations. If this kind of profound interaction with the universe interests you, then you're in luck. This book is for you.

This is a workshop to get you there with the least amount of unpleasantness. You don't need to finish feeling emotionally bruised. Actually, it's meant to be light and fun! I am going to give you the answer right from the start. The answer is *love* . . . but in order to understand its power, you have to choose it first. You have to commit to serve it without even the tiniest fraction of doubt. You will never endure the challenges your intellect demands of you if you don't believe with everything you are that you deserve the fulfillment that will come once you activate the body to participate in love. With the heart, the mind, and the body in harmony, you can face the challenges that life brings your way.

Throughout my life, I have used art and creative energy to help find that harmony. With each chapter, I bring you a challenge to help kick-start your own creativity.

It can feel next to impossible to get out of your own head when you are going through difficult times, but the universe is out there. These challenges are intended to shake you out of your routine and help you open up to the possibilities around you. It's important to be able to let yourself play. All these exercises are intended to help you understand yourself more deeply, and learning should be fun!

Over the course of our adult lives, we lose the sense of wonder that comes preinstalled when we are born. Our curiosity gets dulled over time, but it's not impossible to reignite it. Your creativity can inspire you to reconnect with your self, your sense of wonder, and the people around you. With the heart, the mind, and the body, we can learn to listen, look, and learn.

I want you to keep in mind three things as you read this book. They're the most important things, especially if times are difficult—these are your superpowers that will get you through good times just as well as hard times, especially if you approach them with love. Are you ready?

Joy. Kindness. Truth. It sounds simple, but simple isn't always easy. While practicing all three in your daily life can be a challenge, these are the elements that will help you open up to the *more* that's out there in the world around you.

I hope this experience inspires enthusiasm for learning how to activate your personal superpowers. I promise you, the more you participate in the practices of joy, kindness, truth, with love, the more you will trust the value of your intellect and your body.

MORE

Take the bait
Fly to nowhere
Who do you think you are?
Special is ego
Unworthy the same
If we don't see the challenge
We remain tame.

The system controls us
Our stupidity a trap
It's time for the call out
A universal slap.

Wake up, folks trapped in the shell
So afraid to be broken
We're told we'll see hell
What a farce.

And what if we see, see what?
Something ugly? So that's not for me?
So, say goodbye and turn away
Fear is not a place of obedience to stay.

Ever evolving, moving in turn
Say yes to the notion, we are here
Here to learn. Dark's just a country

Nothing goes in without our approval,
Not children anymore—our choice
Is what we stand for.
Light is my Anchor. I'll help it be yours. I'll
Reflect it in my actions, the strength of yours.

There is nothing we cannot overcome
If it went in feeling bad, we know where it came from.
I will help release you from the burden
From which you come. This darkness
Is like a wave. Say okay, then send away.

Bow down to others, they mirror yourselves.
The Judgment of others is where we
Drown.

Are you ripe or are you vacant?
Sitting in holes of discontentment?
Seeking a win of false containment?
Our ideology has no sustainment.

Contagious wonder changes the whole
Does it matter to you? Do you have a role?
Here's a proposition, take control!
Your Universe awaits you, dare to unfold.

I can't say that I can't do this
The commitment to love offers bliss
Test my crazy, crucify my wrong
I've lived too long to not sing my song.

Risk takes courage, courage is strength.
To know yourself is the biggest risk you take.

My name is Anne. I am the same as you.
You've been told before. I say it again
The God that's in me is the God that's in you.

The triangle of consciousness is a simple equation
Heart mind and body equal in passion
Not one or other has greater power
Equal in strength, serving one another.
There is *no one* greater than any other.

CLARITY:
A DICTIONARY OF WORDS,
USED SPECIFICALLY

Words are meant to build bridges that connect our minds and hopefully begin an open channel to communicate for the purpose of understanding. We can all look these words up in a dictionary, but I am using them in a specific way in this book, so I want to be sure that you and I are on the same page.

Word + Definition = Foundation for Communication

COMMITMENTS
Decisions we make willingly and with the purpose of union with ourselves or others.

EQUALITY
The acceptance that you are no better or worse than any other person who exists. We all matter.

RISK
An unexplored personal action that does not seek approval.

TOLERANCE
The acceptance that I am not you and you are not me. The first building block to respect.

LEADER
A person who sets an example through action and language.

DISCLOSURE
The act of allowing others to see beyond our skin to the inside. The self that shares.

POSSIBILITY
The curiosity with you and what's next.

CHOICE
The singular intelligence that gives us power.

GUIDANCE
An equal exchange of wisdom: the Knower offering, the Seeker accepting.

DOUBT
The gift that leads to clarity. By questioning the world around us, we arrive at our own truths.

RESPECT
The only introduction. Treating people as *people*, with all the thought and care with which we would treat ourselves.

PERSPECTIVE
The exact distance between you and the truth.

PERCEPTION
The story we tell about our distance from the truth.

WORTH
The concept that keeps us in a system where *more* or *less* exists through perception.

KEY
A surprise clue worthy of our attention.

PRACTICE
The act of making our actions reflect our belief.

BELIEF
Our inner engine that drives us forth regardless of what anyone else thinks.

RESPONSIBILITY
Knowing that you got yourself to the moment you're in.

HABIT
The behavior we adopt when we'd prefer to ignore what's next.

PARTICIPATION
The choice we make to engage others that combines our energy with theirs and creates a third energy that wouldn't exist otherwise.

FEELING, also known as EMOTION
The expression both outward and inward that is our connection to a person or thing.

ACTIVE PARTICIPATION
The antidote to being stuck in our emotions.

GOOD WEIRD
A description that was given to me by my son that has empowered me over the years.

CRAZY
A generally accepted term for what exists outside our comprehension.

INTENTION
The determination of how we want our words, our actions, and our theories to take effect.

PURPOSE
The guide, the goal, the rule book that keeps us focused on our destination.

SUPERPOWER
An innate ability that engages all possibility.

RITUAL
The agreement in word, thought, and deed that gives you structure, foundation, and purpose to serve its belief with action.

RESISTANCE
The pause within ourselves that structures our ability to wait for clarity to arrive before making any decision.

CHAPTER ONE

Stretch

LESSON: YOGA or
MEDITATION MIGHT FIX IT

I think one of my agents put it most succinctly when he described me as "a wild animal set free from its cage" when I first descended upon Hollywood. I will never know if that was meant as a compliment. I also heard them describe me as a white trash version of Gwyneth Paltrow—that one I was certain was not a compliment. I had never really heard any encouragement from my parents other than, "She cleans toilets well." At 22, coming from nearly four years on *Another World* in New York, I decided that I had a fifty-fifty shot of making it as an actress in Hollywood, and those were pretty good odds—better than I had previously. I also decided I would never read a review or become overly concerned with opinions of me.

Simply put: Why ask what you don't want to know?

When you're an actress, there are certain demands placed on you. I often heard "shut up and look pretty" at the beginning of my career. I immediately adopted a Red Bull–and–cigarette diet . . . and what was the first part of that again? Oh yeah! "Shut up." I've always had a confusing relationship with that one. No matter how hard a lot of different people have tried along the way, I just can't seem to keep my mouth shut.

Like, for example, the time soon after I moved to LA when I met Oliver Stone at his casting office. I had no idea who he was then, but whoever he was, he didn't look up when I walked into the room, and that seemed rude.

What he was looking at was a large glass desk with a lot of paper spread across it. But there were spaces between the piles, so I assumed the jigsaw puzzle on the table could be put on hold for at least a second while I introduced myself on *his* level. Or at least the level he was willing to see *me* on.

I crawled under the desk, backward bending and on my knees. I waved from beneath the glass, the only place I thought he would see me, between pages of résumés and headshots. "Hi! I'm Anne." I smiled. "What's *your* name?"

He would not be the first director of his stature (I didn't know what that meant, but they yelled it a lot during the feedback phone call) to tell his assistant, who would tell *his* assistant, to make certain that I was never allowed to audition for him again.

Allow me to clarify: he had *no reason* to take my not knowing his name or who he was personally. If I had known, I would've complimented him for sure. But I didn't know anybody who had stature at the time. I am a white-trash girl from Ohio who was raised in Atlantic City, with one book on our shelves: the Bible. Furthermore, the Bible was taken as literal truth and not considered a metaphor in any way.

My apology to the magnificent Mr. Stone; I wouldn't have known his name if he were God himself.

My agents strongly suggested yoga and meditation. I nearly barfed at the suggestion, then blurted, "You obviously know *nothing* about me if you think *that's* going to help *this*." I quickly learned that in Hollywood language, *strongly suggest* means *do it or we won't represent you anymore.*

First, what's yoga? And isn't meditation a rich-person sport? Would they want me to eat nothing but kale? Cutting out my cheese fries is a sacrifice, folks. Besides, I was young and struggling. My agents might have suggested yoga, but they didn't offer to pay for it.

The waiting room of a yoga studio was purgatory. I mean, was the intent to set the bar so high that you'd accept you'd never achieve the Cindy Crawford–like perfection of the five half-naked supermodels behind the check-in counter? Apparently, everyone but me got the memo to wear Birkenstocks only the night before. Not good. I felt painfully out of place in a space where people wore underwear and tossed back granola like Tic Tacs.

My choices were: quit acting or sit my ass on the last corner available on the pickup bench where half-naked, sweaty, gorgeous yoga-ers were massaging each other's overly stressed calves and perfectly painted toes, giggling about Shah-vas-en-aaaahz and ooooohing and aaaaahing all the while. Gag. No, *really*—gag!

"Is that . . . ?" I sniffed the air. What was that horrible smell?

Suddenly, the attention was *all* on *me*. Why were their noses turned up *so* snottily? Then it occurred to me that maybe, just maybe, it *could* be that the *odor* emanating from my recently yanked-off, sweaty, maybe-a-little-poopy sneaker *could* be the reason. No, I hadn't stepped in shit, but the Laundromat was inconvenient, and wearing the same socks the third day in a row . . . ? Okay, yes. Bad choice on my part. Very bad choice.

In that perfectly humiliating moment, Pencil Patty behind the desk, the Cindy Crawford look-alike, called my name. And not *cheerfully*, I might add.

"Anne? *Anne?*" I wanted to deny my name. "You with the shoe." (Everyone had cleared the bench and was gathered by the open window.) Pencil Patty wasted no time, nor humiliation, nor privacy—

"Your card didn't go through. Do you have a different one? Or cash? Better if it's cash." She glared at me.

"Me?" I didn't even bother, just pointed to my brain, as if *it* could explain. I slipped the reeking twenty-dollar bill from the underside of my by-now-discolored, sweaty-shoe secret money compartment. (Until now! Now everyone knows I hide my cash in my shoes.)

Then I flung that fucking twenty at her as if I had no care in the world about the fact that it was *my last twenty bucks in the world! And I still don't give a shit!*

I *wish* I had screamed. I *wish* I had done that. That is *not* what I did. *I* started wondering if I really needed an agent after all. Closing my eyes, pondering just how broke I was exactly . . . Then something snapped. I opened my eyes. It was Pencil Patty's fingers, one hand snapping, her other hand holding what looked to be a bill, my twenty-dollar bill—but at closer glance, it was, in fact, a *five*-dollar bill.

"We've all decided this one's on us."

After Pencil Patty had put my mat directly in the exact *center* of the *front* row, to be able to see me better, it being my first time and all, *I ripped every single muscle in my body* to prove—to *who*, really? Patty? The class at my back? Myself? *What?* That I could overcome the humiliation for the belief in my destination?

I finished the class. I had done what my agents asked me, and despite the initial embarrassment, it hadn't even been that bad. No way was I giving up cheese fries, though! I had opened my mind—I didn't have to change my whole way of life.

PRACTICE: JOY

I f practice is the act of making our actions reflect our belief, then doing the practice is the art and craft of making our belief system a ritual.

Ritual is often associated with a more spiritual, less scientific commitment, like, for example . . . meditation. A ritual can refocus us into seeing the whole of the universe that is offered and gaining the thrill of combining the best that both logic and spirituality can offer, to forward both. The gift is that we don't need to choose or reject either force of nature, to the exclusion of one. Imagine that! Let's come to embrace the next grandeur, a combo platter that allows us to be open to the world around us—if we so choose. That's the tricky part.

Truth be told, love is a choice. Truth is a choice. Choice is our greatest superpower and often our most ignored. It's hard to take responsibility for every decision we make, every step we take. How often do we wish, can't someone else do it for us? Well, unless we take care to make our own choices and take charge of our decisions, that's exactly what's happening. We live in that result—unless we change our way of thinking and embrace the possibilities within ourselves: the strength of love, both for ourselves and for those around us. If you approve, continue on.

If you question your security, your defenses, and want to find strength where you feel weakness, this practice of joy can help. Remember: this book intends to ignite the fire in all of us to take our superpowers back. These guidelines and challenges are here to help us get back on track with our hearts and our intelligence. Let yourself shake yourself up!

Love is a superpower. Love is a science. Love is a religion. Love is a reality. Love is a study, a concern, a care, a desire. In fact, love is our truest life-or-death decision once we choose to seek its wisdom, its direction, and its power. Are you ready? Do you want it? Have you asked yourself what love means to you? Love is that big a deal.

I've developed the practice of joy to be in communication with God, the source and core that guides my heart to believe; with the universe and the mind that joins belief and consciousness; and the light, the physical powerhouse that is the active participation of that equal commitment, one with another. Joy is the practice, and the purpose of the practice is love.

I grew up in a very religious household—a restrictive household. My true religion as an adult is found in taking action: in acts of kindness and love to the people around me. There is a difference between organized religion and spirituality. Religion is not a requirement of the practice of joy. I feel connected to a higher power, to the universe around me, which is something greater than myself. At different times in my life, I have had the experience of seeing patterns in my life that pointed me toward a destination, as though my higher power was speaking to me.

In this book, I will use "God" as a shorthand to reference that higher power.

CHALLENGE: LOOK AT YOUR LIFE INSIDE OUT, UPSIDE DOWN, AND BACKWARD

Everything you greet is a piece of the puzzle if you know the picture. But sometimes we resist what we see. Not maybe what you were expecting as the resounding beginning *ka-BOOM* of a practice that promises joy as its destination. Part of the puzzle of the universe is to be offered a conundrum, seemingly impossible to configure logically, and to choose a way to make sense of it. The sole *and* soul purpose of the practice of joy is to fuck with what we think we know by stimulating our hearts to resist our fears. In any given situation you can tell yourself, "Anne would go further!"

As a society, as a nation, as a community, we are asking to join in a communion with something more than what we are alone. *More* can be thought of as anything that we are not. We can be open to the possibility of there being more than all things material, physical, and personal. *More* is the easiest way I define God. If you look around you and you didn't create it—cook it, sew it, or manufacture it—it is more than you. We can choose to take nothing for granted and add to our strength. The moment we try to be attentive to those around us and reach out beyond ourselves, we generate that *more*.

The challenge for this chapter is to ask yourself what

someone has advised you to do that you resisted—and do it anyway. When somebody is telling us to be open to something, we often push it aside, thinking we know better. If we look inside ourselves to understand the why of that resistance, we can prevail with curiosity and explore the *more*. We are suddenly in a world where what we believe is not right for us flips from "not interested" into an adventure.

So go forth. Try not to go on to Chapter Two until you've done something you didn't want to do. I dare you to enjoy it.

Experiment

LESSON: SEXUALLY FLUID

first understood that my life could and would be told in decades rather than years when I was recently on a podcast promoting a project and they introduced me as "Anne Heche: the first 'sexually fluid' person to go public."

Wondering what flavor I might be, being liquid and all, I'd hesitated to define for myself what that meant, exactly, and allowed others to distill for me what it meant for them to define me as such. And what it boiled down to was that I "went both ways" and stood up for the right to do it.

I was more flattered than offended, to be certain. I had so many questions to ponder, and yet for the purpose of the interview, I chose to embrace the intent of the comment, whether it was correct or not, as a compliment. To an interviewer two decades younger than me, I seemed like something that hadn't existed to this generation until I did. And I thought that was pretty cool. It evolved my understanding of the moment I had participated in with a woman named Ellen DeGeneres, with her leadership, that planted the seed that has now blossomed from thought into law. Same-sex marriages are now legal in this country, a right that *did not exist* at the time. There is nothing in my life I am prouder to have participated in—other than childbirth, of course!

This was a moment when I realized that I wanted to participate in demanding equality regardless of gender and making it law. He or she did not matter to me. The first time I saw Ellen, I realized how true that was.

She was a beacon of truth in an electric-blue suit, beaming light across the room at the *Vanity Fair* Oscar party. Embracing your purpose changes your aura. *That's* what Ellen was radiating from head to toe. Her smile was righteous, knowing that what she was doing was held in the esteem it deserved. And I was fluid enough to acknowledge and admire the human being who was accepting the responsibility of communicating that message; and I had the honor of standing by her side for the time she needed me there.

Simply put: exquisite doesn't have gender. Neither does love.

I had driven myself to the *Vanity Fair* Oscar party in my "vintage" Toyota truck with no brakes, wearing a secondhand emerald-green, fake suede car coat, over the only full-length black dress I owned, which had been bought for me by my ex Steve Martin to look appropriate for one or another event. I barely kept myself standing as my first steps onto a red carpet were greeted by photographers calling my name and flashing bulbs toward me, as if they were interested in me. How or why they knew my name was the first question I needed the answer to. Thankfully, I spotted my agent only feet away from the entrance I had stumbled inelegantly through, baffled and clueless.

While she was delivering an explanation, I found myself staring out into a sea of Oscar winners and nominees chattering and congratulating each other. It was a black-tie extravaganza of stature and statues.

"Who is that?" I interrupted. "Can I meet *her*?"

When I was first introduced to Ellen that night, she knew who I was, but I did not have a clue about her, which she found shocking. (Not a shocking statement to tell you that I did not read tabloids or watch entertainment news. Remember, I did not even know who Oliver Stone was.)

I made a direct line over to her and asked why she was beaming so bright. She was surprised I didn't know. Understandably so—she was coming out on national television, on her TV show *Ellen*, and was about to record this monumental episode that same week. Oprah was going to be there!

I was amazed she had her own TV show. She was amazed I didn't know I was the "it girl." With *Volcano*, *Wag the Dog*, and *Donnie Brasco* in the can, there were rumors of me being in contention for an untitled Harrison Ford rom-com . . . There was indeed a reason that the press had been snapping photos of me! Oh goodness, all I ever knew was that I was *not* it. My parents had drilled into me from the day I was born that there was only one true it, and his name was Jesus Christ. And *he* was the only one deserving of our love or adoration.

I wanted to say, "No. No. I'm not. Not it!"

Simply put: I fell in love with a woman! And I was also a woman who hadn't loved a woman before. Voilà: "sexually fluid."

Who could've predicted how my life would change?

A press junket is a promotional event that happens a day or so before a movie premiere—in a hotel, and depending on the size and scope of the movie, how nice the hotel is. This particular one was at the Four Seasons, Beverly Hills, and it was happening soon after I'd met Ellen. We'd been inseparable. Now I was back to work, as *Volcano* was intended to hit it big, knocking the other volcano movie, *Dante's Peak*, out of the park. Press was invited from all over the country to hole up in room after room, to interview the director, producers, and cast, with the results to be released to various media outlets after the premiere. That's where all the clips you see of us being interviewed about how great the experience was, how *blessed* we feel to be a part of the project, come from. And most of it is true. You can always tell when it's bullshit.

It was Thursday. I had asked Ellen to join me for

lunch in the suite they had set aside for me so she could rest after her hugely successful coming out episode had just been taped and would air the following week.

The *Volcano* premier was to be Friday, the very next night. When I entered the room, the first thing I saw was four "suits" standing, arms crossed, staring intently at me, as I walked farther in, and could see: Ellen, sitting in an armchair. There was a heavy silence and the thickest air I had ever walked into. "What's going on?" I asked.

As far as I remembered, I had only invited Ellen to join me. I leaned in to kiss her and was met with pure resistance, as she looked me in the eye and told me I should listen. I straddled the arm of her chair and grabbed her hand, watching intently as the suits shifted, wondering who would speak first. As I held the hand of the woman who had just been featured on the cover of *Time* magazine for her bravery, the first of our time to stand against all odds, for the right to be open about who you love, one of the suits said, "You can't take Ellen to the *Volcano* premiere tomorrow night, Anne."

To which I replied, "What are you talking about?!"

Ellen pleaded with me to understand that they were right. Now was my moment. She had warned me this would happen. "You can't risk it," Ellen said. Then she assured me, with all the love in her heart, that it was okay. We had plenty of time. There was talk of how little we knew of each other, how recently it had been since we met.

"Would you be telling me this if my date was George Clooney?" I asked the suits.

The first time you experience discrimination in the

eyes of the people who represent you is the moment you decide who you are as an artist. I had already decided who I was as a person, but I hadn't been confronted as an artist until this moment. I looked at Ellen. She looked at me, consoling, as if to say, "It's okay. Do this. We'll deal with your conundrum over it when it's over. I'll be waiting for you at home."

"You're fired," was all I could think to say to the suits. "Get the fuck out of here!"

There's not one moment that has defined my life more than that one. Anne, the artist, Anne, the daughter of a man who had hidden his sexuality—we're all the same person. I had no idea how much that one decision would impact my life and what I gave up for that decision.

I also had no idea that it gave so many people the green light to come out of the closet. I am often asked if I regret that moment. I do not.

Ellen and I were ushered out of the movie theater at my premiere of *Volcano* before the movie ended, led through a back entrance, and shoved into our limousine so that there would be no pictures of us taken at the afterparty. The next day, I was fired from a multi-million-dollar-picture deal by Fox, then blacklisted. It would be ten years before I did another studio picture. I felt like patient zero in the cancel culture.

PRACTICE: CARE

Staying committed to your truth can mean disappointments or difficult times. No matter how challenging it gets, it's important to keep in mind that *you matter*. There may be pain or struggles in your life, but you are important, and despite the pain, you can find joy and live in that joy. Remembering that you, too, are a person worthy of love and of good things is key to looking after yourself.

Sometimes it's hard to take care of ourselves the way we should. It's so much easier to treat other people gently. But if you don't take care of yourself, you won't be able to help anyone else. Try to think of yourself the way you would think of one of your friends. If one of your friends was going through difficult times and stress, would you tell them to push through it? Or would you encourage them to take breaks and take care of themself so they didn't burn out? When things are really hard, sometimes it's difficult to take care of yourself at all, to the point where remembering to eat or drink enough water, or take your medicine, or even take a shower can be difficult and feel like an insurmountable problem. Break things down into small steps, and don't yell at yourself if you need to break them down even smaller. It won't help you get anything done, and it will only make you feel bad.

It's also important to remember that you are not alone. While every person is unique, with unique trials, you're not the only person to set your feet to a difficult path. What you are doing, other people have done. What you have suffered, other people have suffered. Whatever you're witnessing, whatever you're wanting or seeking or questioning—there are people out there who have been, if not *exactly* where you are, then in similar circumstances. It can be helpful to reach out and look for others who are experiencing similar difficulties to your own, and in the age of the Internet, it's easier than ever to find online groups for nearly every experience, or resources that can point you to help local to you. You don't have to reinvent the wheel to find ways to help yourself. Other people's experiences can be invaluable. But even if you don't choose to go that route, don't forget that those people are out there and that you are not the only one who's hurting.

The troubles in our lives can make us want to defend ourselves, but even though caring about things involves an element of vulnerability, it also opens you up to joy. So much media and the way people interact, especially online, comes from a culture of indifference and lack of accountability for our actions and words. There are entire genres of media that we consume that elevate cruelty to a form of humor and keep us from engaging fully with the world around us. But our lives are so much richer when we care about the people around us—not just the people we personally know and love, but the people in our communities, both big and small, who need our caring. In this age of cancel culture, we are too quick to write people off. When we shun someone for their opinions, we stop the conversation, and nothing ever changes—it just makes people dig deeper into their one-sided way of thinking.

I invite you to care and be open-minded. Open yourself up to love and transform kindness from a *feeling* you extend to those around you to *actions* that you perform for them. Only by caring can we open ourselves up to the universe, and only by opening up to the universe can we fully experience all the wonders that it holds, the greatest of which is love.

CHALLENGE: PLAY MUSIC

As I have grown as an artist, I have humbled myself to the soul—accepting that others know more than I can ever know on my own.

Music has been a part of my life from my beginning and will be to my end, if that flag shall be raised. I trained myself to grow by listening to music and attempting to feel the beauty, the excellence, and the power that other artists offered me through their music, lyrics, melody, and movement that allowed them the grace to share their divinity through what they give. I started to train myself to move with their song and mouth the words the best I could to attempt to embrace the overflowing cups of glory and delight that so many offer over and over, day after day. I will never reach these heights that these masters of the musical universe have offered, but I can enjoy and learn and pray with them in my workouts and work throughs of my life. Music has healed me, opened me, and taught me. The more I listen, the more I receive. I call this practice my Lip Sync Chapel.

There's something primal and magical about the ability of music to move the human soul. There's a connection between musical notes and the spirit that seems to bypass higher thought and rationality and go straight for human emotion.

There's something magical about making a joyful noise—whether you are a skilled musician with years of practice giving you the ability to coax notes from your chosen instrument, or whether you prefer to only sing off-key in the shower for an audience of one—yourself. Music, both making it and listening to it, lets you tap into the wellspring of emotion that lives within you. It's a gift you can give yourself: a purely emotional experience of music that you're feeling, whether it is technically proficient or simply raw melodic energy.

Take time to delve deeper into the music that moves you. It can be music that makes you want to dance, or that makes you think of the freedom of the open road as you travel, or music about sorrows that can give you an emotional release. I encourage you to make playlists that fit different moods and to let yourself indulge in listening to whichever strikes you at the moment. Letting yourself take in an emotional catharsis can leave you feeling scrubbed clean and ready to feel your feelings anew.

Make time in your day to enjoy music, whether it's a playlist as you walk, something soothing to take you through your commute to work, or singing along to your favorite musical. Music can expand your mind and lift your heart, and if it makes you want to dance—then that brings in the body for the trifecta!

Make a playlist of old favorites, but challenge yourself to find new favorites, too. Listen to songs you've never heard of. Try out a genre you don't usually go for. Open your mind and expand your palate—what you find out about yourself might surprise you.

CHAPTER THREE

Ask, Don't Tell.

LESSON:
AKA: STAR WARS

After I read the script for *Six Days, Seven Nights*, I called my agent and confidently stated, "I can do this with my eyes closed." Only then did I ask, "Who's the guy?"

When the name Harrison Ford came through the receiver, my first thought was "Well, I'll never get this—why did they bother sending it to me?" And when I heard I was going to meet with him the very next Wednesday, along with the director, Ivan Reitman, it was so inconceivable, I couldn't even form the words "No *fucking way!*"

When *Star Wars* was first released, my family was moving its way down the coast from Atlantic City, and we were squatting at a place in New Jersey called Ventnor. My brother, Nathan, worked on the boardwalk at a place that made a delicacy called pizza burgers. They used the leftover mozzarella cheese from the pizzas, and the sauce as well, slopped between bun and burger and voilà! Pizza burgers!

The leftover mashed potato and frozen spinach casserole, which we rotated with milk toast for dinner, was replaced this one night with an extra-special treat. We were going to have pizza burgers and make sugar popcorn to sneak in our jackets to go to the opening of *Star Wars*—the first movie our parents ever let us see in the movie theaters.

That Wednesday afternoon, I could not wait to tell Harrison Ford that he was the star of the very first movie I ever saw. Knowing for a fact that I would never get the role I had so arrogantly said I could play with my eyes closed, I was willing to eat dirt to tell the man I first saw on the big screen, from the front row, that I *illegally* snuck popcorn in my jacket for, that he had changed my life. As I walked into the intimate office theater where he was sitting on the stage, across from Ivan, my pulse sped. Trying to be poised, I blurted out without even bothering to introduce myself first, "You have no idea how amazing this moment is for me! *Star Wars* was the first movie I ever saw! I snuck popcorn because we couldn't afford it—pizza burgers! You're the *first*— My *very first*! *Very first movie!*"

Harrison took a very long pause before saying, "Don't ever tell that story again. It makes me look too old."

The rest of the meeting went something like this:

ANNE: Oh. Okay.

HARRISON: Sit down, you.

(He patted the seat next to him.)

HARRISON: Who are you?

ANNE: I'm Anne Heche. I have no right to be here. But I couldn't waste the chance to meet you.

(Harrison looked at Ivan.)

HARRISON: Well, she's more interesting than most.

(I wondered if that was a compliment.)

HARRISON: Do you want to read a scene or something?

ANNE: Yes! Yes! Can I? Really? Which one?

(Now it was Ivan who chimed in.)

IVAN: The sides, the *scenes*, to read? For the audition?

ANNE: Oh, yeah, I know all the scenes, I know the whole script.

IVAN: You memorized the whole script?

ANNE: (Duh!) Of course! Where should we begin?

(The men looked at each other as if to say—WTF? Who is this person?)

I would think about Harrison's comment, "she's more interesting than most," for years to come. It stuck with me because even though it was odd to say, I realized he was onto something. Being "interesting" was important—and it was good to be different. Since it came to me instinctually, I was going to stay that way.

That very same day, Ellen's episode aired on national

television—making her the first openly gay woman in Hollywood. I felt like the love in my heart infused my reading with Harrison, and the joy of the comedy and the romance necessary for the movie spilled out of me and into the room. The love I felt made me feel strong: more courageous, funnier, sassier! Love made me more myself, and I could tell that Harrison was enjoying it— more for me than for him. He was shining his one-of-a-kind beam of light on me, and I delighted in dancing with it.

Now, if that's not proof that you can make something out of nothing—I don't know what it is.

The passion for my curiosity about love's quest deepened, as I began the experience of life, in that moment, being exactly what you make it. It was for me to decide where to take the opportunities in front of me.

PRACTICE: ATTENTION

Details are the secret specialness someone offers. If we pay attention, they can't help but reveal them. They are the special sauce we all have. They live just below the surface of our armor, adorning us. If you start to pay attention to the world around you and the people around you, you will find connections everywhere you look.

I have never believed I write alone. I write with an open channel to the universe that guides me. I believe I was stripped down enough by my reality that I was open to something—*anything*—that would make my life make any sense at all. I don't believe I am alone in that seeking. I do believe I have been singular in my commitment to choose it over anything else offered. You can open up to seeking in your everyday life. You can pay attention to the universe around you. You can pay attention to *yourself*. Recognize that you matter, that *you* are a subject worthy of your own attention. You matter. Paying attention to the things in your life that bring joy to you and the people around you will always be a subject worth studying.

I have found a life path in my devotion to seeking the truth this universe offers, and my belief that choosing to serve a greater purpose than the self opens doors unequaled to any other power we've been offered.

When you pay attention and look for your connection to the universe and the people around you, you open yourself to the messages that the universe sends you.

CHALLENGE: MAKE ART

An incredible way to connect with the creativity inside you is to make art. You don't have to be da Vinci or Michelangelo to connect with your artistic self. The creative impulse is in all of us, and you don't have to be technically proficient to get joy from the creative process.

In fact, let go of the idea that art must be good. What is *good*, anyway? All you need is a pen and paper and to let yourself loose with whatever emotions you're feeling. Sometimes you don't have words for an emotion, but art allows you to work through it anyway. You can spread paint across a sheet of paper and drop another color and watch the paint spread and get the satisfaction of self-expression without having to put words to what you're feeling.

Let yourself connect with the act of making art. Whether you're drawing, sculpting a lump of clay, or knitting a scarf, let yourself focus on the process. Try something new. Take a painting class or watch a YouTube tutorial about a medium you've never used before. Let yourself find joy in the act of learning, and let yourself connect with the creativity you had as a child.

Simply put: when you open yourself to the creative process, you open yourself to the joy of making something with your own two hands. You connect your mind and body and nourish the creative energy that lives in your heart.

Your challenge, if you choose to accept it, is to set a timer and let your imagination go wild. Take twenty minutes to open yourself to the opportunities for creativity around you. Make some time just for yourself to try to free yourself from your everyday routine and express yourself in a different medium. If you're paralyzed by the choices and the many kinds of art available, here's a creative challenge I often enjoy: fill the page with a drawing and never lift your pen from the paper.

Activation of the creative mind is a game I play with myself. Let yourself enjoy the challenge of activating your mind and hands in a way you don't usually. Resist the critical part of yourself that wants to keep you from letting yourself go. Don't worry about what the final product is going to look like. What's important is the road to getting there and letting yourself get caught up in the joy along the way.

Take a moment to reflect on what you're feeling as you create. Is the critical part of yourself louder than the creative part? What parts of the process are fun? What parts are a challenge? Take the opportunity to listen to yourself and look at what you're doing—it's a chance to learn a little more about yourself. Each time you stretch yourself out of your everyday zone and try something new, you give yourself a chance to make sense out of the things that work for you and discard those that don't.

CHAPTER FOUR

Listen

LESSON: GOD TOLD ME SO

The first time I met God (that I was aware of), I didn't have a choice in the matter. I was thrown down in broad daylight in Manhattan, half a block from the entrance of the Shoreham Hotel, where I was staying to shoot *Donnie Brasco*. I tripped and face-planted between the curb and sidewalk. And when I tried to get up, it felt like an anvil fell on my back, pinning me to the ground. If this has happened to you, you know this is a unique position to find yourself in. Every single pore of my body wanted what I was experiencing to be unreal. My soul was pleading with the cement curb and everything else I was witnessing from that ground to pull me up and out of what I was experiencing. Until I literally couldn't hold the weight.

"Embarrassing" is an understatement. I was afraid of who I was, what was happening, and what (or who) got me there. I was torn between fear, embarrassment, and intense interest and curiosity.

(I paused longer than Harrison had when he first met me, and then I addressed my higher power directly.)

ANNE: God?
GOD: Yes.
ANNE: You couldn't have picked a more . . . private place?
GOD: For what?
ANNE: This . . . conversation?
GOD: You don't receive subtle messages.

I spent the next twelve days in New York in complete submission to the conversation I had with this higher power that day on the pavement. It seemed that the universe was talking directly to me through these kinds of signs. If I listened to the universe and went where it told me, it showed me patterns that helped guide my choices. It showed me reasons and answers. Not every moment of connection with the universe will be so visceral and direct, and not everyone will believe this story, but, if you look for the signs around you, I promise you will find them.

One simple example was that I knew that I wanted to write, but I had not yet begun. During one of these days I passed a store, and it seemed as though something were whispering to me, "Go inside. You will find beautiful leather notebooks."

The store was not a stationer. It was a shoe store. At first glance, you'd think that notebooks, much less such a specific kind of notebook, would be the last thing you'd expect to find. But I trusted my connection with the universe, and the voice of a higher power, so I went inside. No notebooks. Not a single notebook in sight—not even a planner or greeting card.

Nonetheless, I didn't believe that I had come to the wrong place. I walked up to the man behind the counter, who owned the store, and asked if he happened to have any leather-bound notebooks in stock, perhaps in a back room where they weren't obvious to the casual browser.

His eyebrows drew together, and he gave me a startled look.

PROPRIETOR: As it just so happens, I do have some leather-bound notebooks. I've never been able to figure out what to do with them.

ANNE: Well, I know just what you should do with them—you should sell them to me!

He reached under the counter and pulled out a stack of beautiful leather-bound notebooks. They were exactly the kind of thing that I had in mind, and the exact kind of thing to entice a new writer to spill her thoughts. The universe was confirming what my gut already believed: I was on the right track and doing what I was meant to do.

That long conversation with God became like a

portal that has shaped and defined every action of my life from that moment forth. It opened up my creative soul to a world I had not known. It pointed me away from the darkness and abuse that had consumed the first part of my life and gave me a pathway and a message I didn't even know I'd been looking for, that I would embrace forevermore. If it took that much energy from the universe to get me to agree to my life purpose, I would abide. I was sculpted, formed into a person that believed at the end of those days and conversation, in one guiding light: *love*.

Put simply: I was given my purpose.

Purpose has consequences. Like the truth, the agreements I made with myself or the universe had unseen challenges: impossible to ignore, impossible to deny, yet terrifying to embrace. I followed my path—but not without mistakes along the way.

Let me jump forward: April, 2000. Ellen was rebuilding from the ground up from the cancellation of her TV show. She was doing a stand-up tour, and I was her documentarian. It was a job I wanted, but also the only one I was offered at the time.

I'd been labeled "outrageous" because I fell in love with a woman. I had never been with a woman before I dated Ellen. I did not, personally, identify as a lesbian. I simply fell in love! It was, to be clear, as odd to me as anyone else. There were no words to describe how I felt. "Gay" didn't feel right, and neither did "straight." *Alien* might be the best fit, I sometimes thought. What, why, and how I fell in love with a person instead of their gender, I would have loved to have answered if anyone had asked, but no one ever did.

My newness within the sexuality spectrum had been culturally vilified, and my choice to love a person of the same sex as me, even though I wasn't apparently born this way, was a concept that was described at different times by different people as "too outside the box," "too weird," or simply, "sick."

(I'll never forget being on *Oprah* with Ellen in 1997. When Oprah referred to our relationship, she asked me, "What do you think when people say, 'Yuck'?" I don't think this is a question that Oprah would ask today— progress, folks!)

I'd found myself in the exact position I had witnessed with every gay man or lesbian I had ever met. They were cast out for being born different from the norm. And I, in the "everyone deserves to choose who they want to love" zone, was ostracized for being different from both the gay people and the straight people. I didn't yet know that I would come to be a representative for the right to be different. How could I, when I seemed to be "too different" to be either gay or straight? People seemed to want me to pick a side. I thought I already had!

One of the stops along the way of the tour was Washington, DC, where we would be attending, marching, and speaking with many others, on April 30: the Millennium March on Washington for Lesbian, Gay, and Bi Equal Rights and Liberation—one of the biggest protests in American history.

Now when you're at the "Gay March" (which was what they called it back then; at the time, it was more of an umbrella term) on Washington, as a newly bona fide gay activist, and you're at the podium speaking to a minimum of a million flag-waving, rainbow-painted, out-and-proud gay, lesbian, and transgender people and bisexuals, it is *not* the time to be ignorant. *Or* stupid. *Or* arrogant. I was *all* those things.

My first message was simple: "*Come out.*" I then continued, "Straight people, like I was until very recently, need to know who you are, and not all of you wear it on your sleeve. And as someone who lived the first part of my life as 'straight,' I had no idea of the scale of discrimination you face. And we have to do something about it!"

(Duh!) *They were doing exactly that!* That's what the march was all about, Heche! And all million-plus of them were standing proudly together, shouting it from the mountaintops, or in this case the Capitol Steps, the Pentagon, the Lincoln Memorial, the White House, and everywhere in between, "We're here, we're queer, and we're tossing the shame of denying it in the DC dumpsters."

My second message was the real problem. I disagreed that being gay was not a choice. After all, I think choice is power. I had chosen to fall in love with a woman, and I hadn't been with the same sex before.

It was as if I called out, "*Gay can be a choice!* Look at me! I *choose* to be in love with this woman who is essentially the queen of the *you're born this way* message, and I *wasn't* born this way! I just fell in love! Sexuality can be a 'heart thing'!"

I basically said that I just recently became gay, and that I had chosen to when I fell in love with Ellen. In 1993, a study had just come out positing the existence of the "gay gene." That study has never been replicated, and scientists no longer believe there's any such thing, but at the time, LGBTQ+ people were thrilled to have what seemed to be evidence that who they loved wasn't a sin or a moral failing, but literally a part of their genetic makeup as a human being. They could tell their families and loved ones that, no, they couldn't just choose to be with someone of the opposite sex—who they loved was part of who they were!

And then I came along to say that it *was* a choice.

(Open mouth—insert foot.)

I think I got a good dig in about Trent Lott, the senator from Mississippi who made many anti-LGBTQ+ statements over the course of his career, and not wanting to be anything like him—but I had alienated the entire crowd with one statement. They hated me. I had in one fell swoop negated their entire identity, their power in numbers, in the community, fuck! *I had negated their colossal, historic protest.* They were demanding equality for the selves they were born to be. And the truth is, all I wanted to do was applaud each and every one of them.

Yet I had a lot to learn about communicating and expressing this love. I was dedicating my life to figuring out how best to approach the world with love. But I wasn't there yet, and, with the best intentions in the world, I talked over the truth of many people there.

What I wanted to do was join the crowd. Help the fight to love without judgment and further its celebration. And I apologize for any confusion about my intent. But the truth is, I was stating something different. I was proclaiming something I had discovered by falling in love with Ellen, a commitment to living in love, the seeds of which had been planted so many years before on a street in New York City. I learned, for me anyway, that love is a choice. And if you're lucky enough to feel it, give it, and receive it, it gives our bodies a chance to experience what it feels like to be real. We are here on this earth *one* time in *these* bodies. Why *not* enjoy it?

All questions of sexuality aside, last I checked, love is gender-free.

PRACTICE: THE OTHER SIDE

The flip side is a belief. To be as clear as possible, that means: a belief that there is only one power greater than *hate*, and it is *love*: the exact opposite—the flip side.

I believe the power of love is contagious. Hate is a disease that has spread for generations, rotted our system, our societies, our religions, our foundations, with a false prophecy that domination serves community, offers protection, and delivers salvation with *death* as its destination. This disease of hate and abuse cycling through our society must be eradicated. I don't practice organized religion, but can I hear an *amen*!

People fall into the trap of thinking that there's only one way to be, and it's usually whatever they grew up believing. They think in such rigid ways that their minds completely close off to anything that seems outside their understanding. It's this mindset that leads to hating anyone outside whatever their "normal" is. No one can hate every single person who practices a religion they disagree with or loves someone of the same sex. They're individual people and just as human as anyone else. They're as much a part of the universe, and as wonderful and as flawed as all of us are. Blanket condemnation of people outside the norm—whatever that means to the person thinking it—means the person condemning them has begun to think of them as something other than fully human.

It's this kind of thinking that leads to the hatred that calls for attacks on other people, to violence and death. The only way to counter it is to love. The flip side asks that you open yourself to love, and find those corners of reflexive, unthinking hate and iron them out of your mindset. Offer love to the universe and to other people, and you are bringing more light into the world. If you have different beliefs than someone, why not start with what you agree on and make *that* the conversation?

Fuck hate. Honestly, fuck it. Or at least, let's try something else. The flip side: *love*. Acceptance of one another.

CHALLENGE: DANCE FREELY

A lot of the time, you can get caught up in the minutiae of your day-to-day life. It's easy to feel self-conscious when you try to break out of that routine—whether willingly, or, in my case, when I was sprawled across a concrete curb with God trying to get my attention. All too often, we get caught up in the feeling that there are eyes on us—even when we're alone! Especially when we are struggling, or going through difficulties, we get caught up in our heads. Our troubles seem overwhelming, and we spiral into our worries and anxieties, getting trapped in thoughts that won't leave us alone. A good way to break out of that spiral and put us back in touch with the universe outside ourselves is to put on headphones and dance like no one is watching.

Let yourself move. Put on your favorite music and give yourself over to it, whether in a mellow sway to the beat or the kind of wild dancing you usually save for the last song at a wedding reception. Let yourself connect to and enjoy the movement of your body, and let your body get yourself out of your head.

So much of the time, our fears hobble us. Fear of looking silly. Fear of being that person outside the norm. The fear, overall, of *what other people will think*. It's hard to cast off the habit of a lifetime of worrying about how others perceive you, but the reward is freedom to fully be yourself. It takes a lot of practice, but you can

41

take the first steps down that road by letting yourself dance without caring what you look like.

Start in a place where you don't have to worry about other people. Alone, in your living room, or in your kitchen while you cook. Put on a song that makes you want to move and go ahead and do it! It doesn't matter if you don't know how to dance—you're not on a stage, and this isn't a competition. You're dancing for yourself. It might feel silly at first, and that's okay. The point here is to do it anyway. Let yourself enjoy how it feels to move without expectation of what it might look like to anyone else—this is just for you.

You might find yourself wanting to dance with friends, or at a club. Go ahead and do it! Anne says you can. And if you start to worry about how you're dancing, or if people are watching you, remember— you're moving for yourself, and your own enjoyment, not anything else.

And they're probably just as worried about what they look like to *you*.

IF.

If you're doing it, so are they
If you're suffering it, you're not alone
If you're witnessing
If you're wanting
If you're asking
If you're awaiting it
birthing it
seeking it
mourning it
If you're expecting it
If you're missing it
If you're singing it
If you're releasing it
If you're fighting it
You're not the only one
And nor are they

CHAPTER FIVE

Trust

LESSON: *O PIONEERS!*

Without divine intervention, I would've never become an actress. It was something that was hard to imagine, given my childhood. I grew up in such a restrictive household, I didn't have the ability or scope to think of a different path to adulthood than the ones I was told were acceptable.

First of all, as a child, you're unaware that there is a space for something new in the future ahead of you. At least, I was. I had to carve out that space for myself as I went along. It was unthinkable, both to myself and those around me, that I could make a career out of something like acting. But the bigger the resistance, the stronger the path you discover needs to be forged. It's the difference between walking down a paved trail and hacking a path to the future with a machete. The things that seem most obvious to you are met with hesitation and rejection by those around you (and sometimes yourself), and it just simply doesn't make sense to your internal, secret, private agreements along the way.

These agreements are how you shape yourself and the path you choose to take. You make these agreements with yourself. With God. With whatever keeps your clock ticking. These agreements are what make you wake up in the morning and say, "I'm happy to be here. I'll keep doing what I'm doing and believing what I believe in, to make *today* okay and *tomorrow* something I want to wake up to, so I can do it again." It took a lot of signs from the universe to get me to realize that the path I needed to take was the path I was already on. And it can take a lot of time to learn how to use your gifts.

In tenth grade, I was cast in a high school play, Thornton Wilder's *The Skin of Our Teeth*. I was playing the role of Sabina, much to the junior and senior actresses' distress. No tenth grader was to get cast in leading-lady roles. It was the way of the school. It was meant to keep the casting process fair and make sure everyone would eventually have her turn in the spotlight. But I was cast anyway.

I shot out on stage on a wintry night spouting lines I didn't really understand the meaning of—but I said them with feeling anyway.

ANNE/SABINA: Oh, oh, oh! Six o'clock and the master not home yet. Pray God nothing serious has happened to him . . . we would certainly be inconsolable and have to move into a less desirable district.

I should back up and tell you how I even ended up at a prestigious school, one that was known for its theater program. How? Luck . . . ? Fate . . . ?

The day after my father died of AIDS, the *New York Times* declared AIDS a gay disease—essentially outing my father. My family became outcasts of our church community. It was a very difficult time. We were forced to move and ended up in Chicago.

Needing to go back to school, I wandered into Francis Parker, a college preparatory school, by myself one day. I said I had to enroll in high school. The principal informed me that it was a private school. "What's that?" I asked. It was then that she told me it cost money to attend. Well . . . I didn't have any of that. As I started to walk away, she invited me into her office to chat, and I later received a full scholarship. It was truth on my part and kindness on hers that began my life story.

Back to *The Skin of Our Teeth*.

Sabina spews paragraphs of a monologue. Who could have ever predicted that the risk the drama director took in casting a tenth grader would save my life? It turned out that Donna, a casting director for Proctor and Gamble, was laid over because of snow conditions on her way to Los Angeles, looking to cast a part on a soap opera called *As the World Turns*. Jennifer Beals and Daryl Hannah had graduated from the high school

I was attending on full scholarship, and the casting director decided that rather than go to an airport hotel, she would see if that same school happened to have a play performing that night.

When the play ended, with none of my family in attendance, Donna came backstage. Dan, the school director who cast me, told me there was a woman that wanted to talk to me. I was greeted with a respect I'd never experienced, from an adult or anyone. She complimented my performance and then asked if I'd be interested in flying to New York City to screen test for a soap opera.

I said, "Absolutely!" (Beat, beat.) "What's a soap opera?"

(I didn't have a TV. I never had.)

I was flown to New York. I was put in front of cameras. I was shown a studio with sets and actors and makeup rooms. I was offered a role on a nationally televised TV show when I was sixteen years old—and I turned it down.

I lived in a one-bedroom shit-bag residential hotel in Chicago. We had no bank account. No phone but for the hotel phone in the middle of our beds that would ring if the downstairs desk rang up. I slept every night hearing sobs from my mother, who had lost her husband to AIDS and then her son to suicide in the previous six months. My two older sisters were already out on their own. I was underage and could not escape that existence without taking the demons of my life and the responsibility I felt to heal them with me. I didn't feel I could leave my mother, and she certainly wasn't going to let me.

There are many reasons why I believe in God. The fact that, not long after the initial offer, the executive producer of *As the World Turns*, John Whitesell, had moved over to a show called *Another World*. He called me on the hotel phone exactly two weeks before I was to graduate high school, and asked if I might be willing to come to New York City again and audition for a part on his *new* show. He remembered why I had turned down his first offer, and this was a new beginning. The truth was my mother would not allow me to leave the first time I auditioned, but I was eighteen now.

John told me, "You'll be an adult once you graduate. You can make your own choices."

He flew me to New York. He tested me for two different characters. He cast me as Vicky and Marley Love. I won an Emmy. John gave me a path out of the life I had been born into.

After four years on *Another World*, I determined that I would never have real security and independence unless I pursued something "normal" that could be a career. I was accepted into Parsons School of Design to study architecture, my other passion. I was to begin attending the week after my contract playing Vicky Hudson and Marley Love on *Another World* was over. I had done over half a *thousand* episodes of television. You'd think that would've sunk in as something meaningful, perhaps a road to a destination. Not for me. *I* decided I needed to go back to school. To prove to myself: *I am worthy of something!* I decided I needed a degree of some sort. Any sort.

Every single person who had worked with me for four years was gobsmacked over my decision. "Go to Hollywood!" was the mantra they were shouting, but it was lost on me. Two weeks before my departure, my favorite producer, Susan Strickler, handed me a novel on my way out the door after shooting all week, through Friday night so that it was now early morning, heading into Saturday's sunrise.

Put simply: I don't read novels. It isn't anything against the form! It's just a lot of very dense information to take in, in long blocks of type on the page, and my brain doesn't seem to want to process that way. Scripts saved my life. They were written in short paragraphs. I could see them, understand them, and teleport them into my brain, which was necessary, because since I was playing twins, I had up to sixty pages of dialogue a day. Half was one character, the other half the other. As I've said, I was never allowed to read as a child. We had one book in the house. It was the Bible. I had to memorize verses every week. Other than that . . . it was me and my imagination.

ANNE: What's this?
SUSAN: A novel.
ANNE: Oh my, oh no. What novel?
(The novel was Willa Cather's *O Pioneers!*)
SUSAN: You'll like it. I promise.

ANNE: Me and "pioneers"? Hmm. I doubt it.

Later that same day, I sat at my kitchen table. Alone with my dog Sammy, as I almost always was on a weekend, I opened this "novel" Susan had promised I would like. I had barely gotten past the title page when the phone rang. It was my agent.

JOANNE (Agent): Sorry to bother you on a Saturday, but an opportunity has presented itself for you to play the best friend of Jessica Lange—
(I interrupted.)
ANNE: Wait. What? I'm not acting anymore.
JOANNE: I know. I get it. But it's Jessica Lange.

If there was one actress I could claim as an idol, after seeing *Tootsie*, it was Jessica. So, suddenly I was interested.

JOANNE: It's shooting next week in Nebraska, and it's a really good project, and you may want to consider reading it. (I was waving the book in my face for air as she continued.)
JOANNE: It's called *O Pioneers!* and they're really interested in reading you.

Are you fucking kidding me?
I stopped fanning my face. I looked at the title of the book in my hand: *O Pioneers!* If ever there was a sign . . . you can't make this shit up!

Cut to a week later with me sitting on the bed of a Motel 6 in Nebraska. Having spent the day on set filming *O Pioneers!*, as I was eating a cheeseburger and unwinding, I learned that I won an Emmy for playing the twins, Vicky and Marley Love, on *Another World*. I picked up the phone and called JoAnne.

ANNE: Does this mean I'm supposed to be an actress?

JOANNE: Yes, Anne. I think it does.

That's the universe winking at you, at all of us. Who chooses to engage and take flight? All we can do is smile and say: okay, I accept.

Put simply: the rest is history—or herstory, as I like to say.

PRACTICE: FOCUS

Without even noticing it, you can fall into a rut in your life and get lulled by your routine and, perhaps, the fear of uncertainty and change. It's important to practice focus in your day-to-day life. It's all too easy, without even meaning to, to start to sleep-walk your way through your daily routines. Our entire lives, we develop programming that tells us to behave in certain ways. It comes from our parents, in large part, but also our schooling, our friends, and the messages we get from media and advertising. The world of *normal* is used as shorthand to convey ideas about how we should be and what families look like, or what success should be. Some of your programming might tell you that it is weird or unusual to be a certain way, but that way is your truth. For me, my programming would've said that I should bet on a sure thing and pursue a career in something traditional. It's hard to break into acting, and even when you do, it can be a career with dramatic ups and downs. There are no sure things. But I listened to what my heart was telling me, not all the messages that had been shaping me since my childhood.

You need to focus on what is true and beautiful in the world around you to keep yourself from missing the wonders that the universe has to offer. Listen to your heart and think with your mind to keep yourself from just accepting the world around you as it's presented to you. You can step out of other people's expectations and find what is meaningful to you specifically. It isn't always what you might think! Pay attention to yourself and focus on your own reactions to the things that happen in your life, and how you feel about them. Only by listening to yourself can you find your own purpose for the practice and bring your presence to the present. You are present for a reason, and that reason is joy. You can find what that means to *you*. Only you are the arbiter of your own happiness. Only you know what success, or family, or love, looks like to you.

We know what we see. We can focus on our *selves* and home in on our own truths. And by living to align with our truths, we can find happiness in the practice of joy.

CHALLENGE: WEAVE TAPESTRY

The threads that connect us to the universe and other people are all around us. They are the unseen connections that we draw as we go about our lives. We can choose to prioritize and nourish the connections with people and places that make us feel better. We can look for patterns around us.

What makes us feel good? What leaves us feeling not-so-good? These can be places, people, or activities. Once you look for the patterns around you, you can start to recognize how they affect you. And when you choose the practice of joy, you put the purpose in the practice. Pay attention to the tapestry you are weaving around you in the things you choose to do, the places you choose to go, and to the people you surround yourself with. These are the warp and the weft of your life, and you can begin to intentionally weave yourself a joyful existence.

Your challenge for this chapter is to start to think consciously about the tapestry you weave. Take a piece of paper and jot down the people and activities in your life that make you feel good and those that make you feel less good. Also write down things you want to try but haven't yet—you can mark those with a question mark. Maybe you want to incorporate a routine of stretches into your morning right after you wake up. Try it and note how it makes you feel. Perhaps you'd like to make a habit of an evening walk after dinner, because you've noticed that it makes you feel good—and if there's a nearby park that always makes you feel happy to walk through, why not combine the two? If drawing or coloring or woodworking brings you joy, make a space in your life to include and embrace that.

Conversely, if there are activities or people in your life that are detrimental to your joy, how can you minimize that time or make it more enjoyable? If you don't like doing dishes or folding laundry, can you enliven those tasks by listening to music or a podcast or watching a show while you do them? If you have an unpleasant person that you can't entirely avoid, perhaps a coworker or relative, can you practice drawing a boundary or changing the subject when they begin to engage you in ways that make you feel worse? Keep a journal so you can see how trying out this conscious shaping of your tapestry makes you feel, both at the moment you engage and over time.

Consciously categorize the areas of your life so you can be aware of the patterns you are weaving, and culture your most satisfying and joyful life.

CHAPTER SIX

Dare

LESSON: LIFE'S MOST EMBARRASSING MOMENTS

I was bare-assed and feeling sexy. It was fair to say the movie I was filming was my biggest movie yet. I was absolutely thrilled and over the moon to be working with Demi amaze-balls Moore and my on-screen partner in crime: the exquisite Mr. Alec Baldwin as the film's villain. The movie was *The Juror*, and as written, *his* character fucks *my* character's brains out after a little light stalking before forcing her to kill herself.

(Of course, his character comes first, before he forces her to kill herself. He wouldn't want to miss out on a good time just because he's planning her death.)

ALEC: I'll fuck the shit out of her and then threaten her. As far as my character's motivation goes, what could make more sense than that?

(So he said to the director.)
ANNE: Absolutely.

As we were in the makeshift dressing rooms on either side of the bed, Alec poked his head around the curtain and said:

ALEC: Heche!
(I poked my head out.)
ALEC: It'd be way more interesting if we come into the sex scene already in the middle of it, don't you think?

The patch of underwear they gave me for filming was just shy of a Band-Aid. It was meant to cover me enough to keep the sex scene from being a little too realistic, without showing up on camera. Alec had started screaming and panting and bouncing while getting sprayed with water to look like he was sweating. We needed to look tousled and like we'd been exerting ourselves—like we were in the middle of the world's absolute sexiest sex. How could I say no?

I jumped out of the dressing room and started jogging in place as water bottles sprayed me from head to toe. It was just coincidence that my Band-Aid began slipping at the exact second we heard the director call out, "Action!" But I was a professional, and the show must go on, so I ignored it.

We leaped onto the bed feverishly, acting this

tarnished scene with abandon, giving the camera our all. Then the director yelled, "Cut!"

I went back to my corner to be wiped or powdered, I didn't care. Whatever they needed for the scene. Alec started jogging in place; I started jogging in place. He got more spray, I got more spray, and as one of those dissolving mints was being gently put onto my tongue by a lovely wardrobe assistant leaning in too closely, she whispered subtly into my ear:

ASSISTANT: Do you by any chance have your period? Can we get something for that?
(My pace slowed to a halt.)
ASSISTANT: Sometimes sexual arousal can stimulate the ovaries, causing a premature menstrual cycle.
(Seriously?!)

At this point, let me remind you that I was naked except for the tiny scrap of the Band-Aid, which did nothing to halt the flow. Apparently I was bleeding buckets of blood, because in half a turn of my head, I saw the entire crew aiding and abetting the frantic de-sheeting of the bed I just *bled* on. There was *no way* it hadn't gotten all over Alec. Blood was *everywhere*.

Every single person on that set, it seemed, was spraying and wiping. They brought out Windex. They brought out Shout. If they'd had bleach, I'm sure they would have brought it, too. They were trying anything and everything to get my blood off him. Then, I heard:

ASSISTANT: Relax. Anne. Relax.
ANNE: Oh! Okay!

You try relaxing in a moment like that!

I knew at that moment that I needed to look down and face the truth. It was *not* going to be good news. I bit the bullet—I was red colored, as though I'd been splashed with paint from head to toe, and it was *drying* on me.

I was rushed to the real dressing room shower. Yikes. I wondered how fast the news had traveled. Were Demi and whoever told her laughing at me, and how hard? If so, it would be deserved! I couldn't be mad at an entire crew on a multimillion-dollar movie, snickering behind and in front of my back, not after my body had betrayed me like that. They couldn't help it. Who could?

This was the worst possible actor's nightmare, because it was real! I had just menstruated all over Alec Baldwin and decimated the *one* set of sheets they had. I couldn't blame the set dressers for not having a backup plan in case the actress, supposedly *professional*, bled all over everything in the midst of the first take.

They couldn't even get one take in the can, because the sheets wouldn't match. We had to wait for the emergency errand runner to go buy some while we were getting cleaned up.

ASSISTANT: (in a very quiet mumble) This might take a minute.

It is shocking that I didn't walk straight out of the studio and throw myself in front of a bus. The life of an architect was looking pretty good at this moment.

Back on set after what felt like an eternity, I looked at Alec across the freshly made bed. Finally, as he was beaming a broad smile at me and chuckling, he said:

ALEC: Let's make the next take *hotter*. Agreed, Heche?

He started jogging. I started jogging. And yes, it was even hotter than the first. So hot, in fact, they didn't need another take.

That would be the first time Alec had my back. Years later would be the second, when he insisted that I be his Lily Garland to his Oscar Jaffe, on Broadway, in the screwball comedy *Twentieth Century*. I will always be grateful to him for ensuring that I had this amazing, most joyful opportunity on Broadway that was so much fun to play, which garnered me a Tony nomination.

Within the last few years, Alec came on our podcast, *Better Together with Anne & Heather*. I talked to him about this story (even though Heather made me promise I would not bring up the horrific event! I think she was more embarrassed for me than I was for myself). He did not even remember the mortifying details of the story all these years later. He only remembered that lunch was called early—he did not remember why. It's highly possible that your *most* embarrassing moments are way more monumental to you than anyone else.

Think of it this way: bare-ass embarrassing situations can change the course of your life, provide a funny story for you to tell, and are oftentimes not as embarrassing as you may think. (Although, I do think we can all agree mine was pretty bad.) Take the dare!

PRACTICE: GENEROSITY

"The more you give the more you get." Really? We've all heard it, but what does that really mean? And is it true?

Let's start with a meditation. A moment to pause and ask ourselves when we feel most surprised. And further, how much are we most surprised by how much joy we feel? By accident, it just arrives. When was the last time you were surprised by how happy you felt? Was it something you did for yourself? Did someone else make you feel it? Was it spontaneous? Was it constructed? Planned?

Is a joyous surprise something we think about giving another? If not, why not? Seems easy enough. But is it? How much time in our day do we spend thinking about what we can do to make people feel good because of something surprising we choose to do for them, just to make them feel good, simply because we can?

Life has a lot of demands. Get this, do that, pay for this, buy me that. Be this, fix that, I want this, and I can't get that. So there's a lot in front of us that makes us confront the issue of what we *have* and what we have *not*. What someone is *doing* for us and what they're *not*. How we're *received* and how we're *not*. What's going *right* and what's *not*.

What if we took half or even a quarter of the amount of time that we spend working on the demands, required of ourselves or the others around us, and thought about how we could surprise ourselves or another with a treat? A joyous offering? A pleasurable gift? A kind word or just simple appreciation—something unexpected that makes someone or ourself feel better just because.

We can't take away life's demands to do, or be, or provide, or perform something to ourselves or another. But we can substitute some of the time we spend focused on those demands, giving ourselves and others a little more time spent in bringing a bit of joy to the moment: to a dinner companion cackling with laughter when you tell a joke. To a coworker when you bring them a homemade cookie. To a spouse who didn't expect a wildflower bouquet or a night on the town. To a partner who didn't expect to arrive and see you in lingerie.

Love is a practice. It is an art. Take time to practice bringing joy to the world around you. Even the smallest gestures can resonate with kindness.

CHALLENGE: LAUGH FIRST

So many times as we make our way through our lives, we get caught up in more turbulent emotions. Sometimes we get hung up on what our own actions or predicaments might look like from the outside, and our default reaction is to feel embarrassment or shame. Sometimes, things are challenging, and it seems like just when one challenge is resolved, a new one crops up. Sometimes it seems like we just can't catch a break.

It's all too easy to get bogged down in those emotions, but as I ask you to engage in the practice of joy, I invite you to laugh first.

Sometimes you can't. Sometimes things really are so dark that you can't find any humor in them. But sometimes, the humor in a situation is the silver lining on the side of dark storm clouds. And sometimes, a situation is simply embarrassing, and the shame that you feel about it can be transformed into seeing the ridiculous side of things—like when you've just bled on a coworker and are *certain* everyone is laughing at you. It's okay to look for what's funny!

Life is full of enough tears already. So often, our go-to emotions are of anger or sadness. You can't always control what you feel, but you can retrain your brain to find the joy in a situation rather than dwelling on the aspects that feel negative.

I'm not saying not to feel your pain. There are things in life we can't control that hurt us: other people's actions. Deaths of loved ones. Illness or mental health. But there are other situations where we can choose to let a minor annoyance derail us, or we can reframe it as something a little easier to handle.

As you go about your day, I challenge you to rewrite the story. If someone is late meeting you or you're stuck in the checkout line behind someone who cannot complete the transaction because they are busy on their phone, try to come up with a story that puts their actions into context, to give you more patience and understanding. Cast your mind back into the distant past. What's something that seemed terribly embarrassing or frustrating at the time but has become a story you've told your friends for their amusement? Take that energy and apply it to other incidents in your life until they no longer have the power to make you cringe—only to laugh.

More importantly, if you feel annoyance over something trivial, or if embarrassment has made you feel like every eye in the room is on you, try to think of how you might tell that story to a friend later on in a way that shifts the focus from your negative feelings to find the humor in the situation.

Cultivate a sense of the ridiculous. The easier it is for you to laugh, the easier it is to find joy. Friendships and relationships where you and the other person can make each other laugh are to be cherished. Nourish those connections and the joy they bring you. It'll make all your joy easier to find.

CHAPTER SEVEN

Share

LESSON: MY TEACHER

The first scene I had with Harrison Ford, I was on a beach I had been helicoptered onto. (It's still amazing to me that I even get to write that sentence . . .)

Okay, so, the very first scene we filmed of *Six Days, Seven Nights* was the two of us. Basically, the whole movie was just us. We were standing face-to-face, and after *he* had approved *his* close-up, the cameras were now turned onto me. It was time for *my* close-up. Ivan Reitman, the director, yelled, "Action!"

I said my lines. And Harrison, immediately after Ivan yelled, "Cut!" looked at me and said:

HARRISON: Anne, only look in *this* eye.
(He pointed to *one* eye. I was confused.)
ANNE: What do you mean?

HARRISON: You want to be a movie star? The camera is here.

(He pointed to the camera over his shoulder that was pointing at me.)

HARRISON: So look into my *left* eye when you speak.

(The camera was on the right.)

ANNE: I can't do that. I want to see all of you. I mean, all that I can see in your eyes. Both of them!

(I was pointing at his eyes, trying to make him giggle.)

HARRISON: I get it. Soap opera "acting." You want to be a *movie star*, you'll need to understand where to look to deliver your message.

(Was that an insult? I mean, the first part of it certainly was. But the second part...I wasn't sure.)

ANNE: (Attempting an agreement to agree to disagree . . .) Okay, whatever, right? You do it *your* way, I'll do it *mine*.

HARRISON: (Super cheery) Nonsense. We'll do it your way!

Harrison gave Ivan the cue to start rolling the film. This is an artifact of the olden days, when digital didn't even exist in film, and the physical film strip had to be started. A lot has changed since then!

Ivan yelled, "Action!" again. I opened my mouth to speak, and *this* is what I saw: Harrison Ford, lifting his hand to cover his *right* eye, making it impossible for me to look anywhere else but into his *left* eye if I wanted to connect.

Single-handedly, Harrison Ford taught me how to

perform for the camera. He helped me calm my energy and translate it onto film in a way I hadn't had to as the twins on *Another World*. Day after day, scene after scene, I was led, by the biggest movie star on the planet, to become *more*. It wasn't just talent and acting my truth—it was how to *express* it through the camera lens so that everyone watching could receive it.

No one could have helped me as much in that situation as Harrison did. He *chose* to help me, and I'll always be grateful.

PRACTICE: BE YOU

If there is any message I have received in my life that makes this book essential to write and share, it is that love is *not* a secret.

But just because it's not a secret, that doesn't mean its arrival comes easy. In fact, it is the most challenging, surprising, compelling, blatant conversation and education. It's hard to get rid of all the garbage we are fed and bombarded with and find out about what life really is, that could never be imagined or explained, until you embrace the chance to accept the execution of *more*. You are present for a reason. You can resist the programming that society instills in you and forge your own path.

Simply put: Life is your own.

I don't want *my* life for you. I want *your* life for you. I've been given an experience of feeling God. I've denied what I was taught. I've turned left when I was told to go right, I've cleaned toilets, and I've starred in movies. All to find out what love is. All because I asked for it.

You can ask for it, too. You can look within yourself and find your own truths. Look for what brings you joy—and keep your mind open. Sometimes the way you're used to isn't the best way. If you're fortunate enough to have someone who's been there before reaching out to guide your path, the way Harrison helped elevate my acting to a new level, let yourself be open to the possibilities.

But at the same time, stay true to what you know about yourself. We know what we see—that is to say, your intuition about yourself is the strongest force. Trust your gut. Let yourself stay open to opportunities around you, but always listen to yourself. You know what you know!

CHALLENGE: CULTIVATE STRENGTH

Cultivating strength is resisting the ideas you've been programmed with your whole life. Cultivating strength is finding the people who nourish you and support you in your time of need. Strength is also looking for ways you can help others in their time of need. Look for how you can help, and take what you learn from helping others, when the stakes aren't quite so personal, and use it to help navigate your own life.

Make of yourself a rock on which flowers can bloom. Meditate on the things that you *survived* so you can examine the things you learned and how you got through them. So when you're facing difficulty ahead of you, you can think about how you got through the last hard thing, and what you learned from that. Think about mistakes you made, and treat yourself gently, because that, too, is part of your learning process. No one gets through this life unscathed, and no one gets through without making mistakes. But you don't have to let your mistakes define you, and you don't have to let them weigh you down. You can acknowledge them, and learn from them, and give yourself kindness and grace as you prepare to face your next challenges. Sometimes when you don't know how to get through, you can let the higher power of the universe move through you. You don't have to have all the answers at once; you can just keep putting one foot in front of the other as you move forward.

Another source of strength is the relationships of the people you love. These can be family relationships, friendships, romantic partnerships, the bond of a parent and a child—these relationships support and inspire you. I talk often about the support of my "chosen family"—the people that I *chose* to consider family; very strong love and support is certainly not limited to the people you were born related to. They can help you get through hard times and remind you of what's important in your life. If things are difficult, and you're mired in negativity, try to extend to yourself the same kindness and grace that you would give your most important people, because you deserve that kindness, too. You are worthy of it.

Visualization: give yourself a practice run before you face a difficult situation. Walk yourself through the steps that you will need to take and imagine yourself coming out in your desired outcome. This gives your brain a chance to do a dry run of the reactions you might have, so it won't be such a shock when you actually experience them. You are giving yourself a chance to test out the things that might happen and to react to them in a time and place that is safe and as stress-free as you can allow yourself.

There's also strength in flexibility, in letting yourself bend and adapt to the challenges you face. Open yourself to the universe and let the signs and patterns that you see there reinforce your strength. Sometimes the best way forward isn't the most obvious. Let yourself change plans and keep your mind aware that there are other paths.

I challenge you to take time to think about your strength. What are the strengths you're aware of? What are areas you feel lacking in? Think of ways you can bolster yourself, and be kind to yourself as you do it. You wouldn't yell at yourself for not being able to pick up a three-hundred-pound barbell if you've never lifted weights before. Mental strength is like physical strength; you have to develop it over time. Start thinking of ways to keep going on when you might not want to—maybe your costar told you your action was too soap opera–ish for the movies and told you to only look at one of his eyes and covered the other one so you couldn't do anything else. You just might find you're already stronger than you think.

CHAPTER EIGHT

Persist

LESSON: TRUTH

After my father's funeral, the cause of his death was labeled AIDS: the Gay Disease by the *New York Times*. Instantly, people like me and my family became like a new kind of leper. You could've been a distant cousin of someone infected, and if you had been or might be in their presence, you could have "caught it"—or people seemed to think you certainly would "catch it," just from being in the same room. People were afraid to shake hands, much less eat with or hug someone who might have been infected.

I had been sexually abused as a child by a man who had now died of a disease that could infect others. And no one knew how exactly how the disease spread. No one knew where it had come from.

Hepatitis was bandied about. All I knew was that

the only doctor visit I'd had in my life was to test me, at six years old, to see if I was a carrier. And now, I was being told by the second doctor I had ever seen, that I would have to wait *nine years* (minimum) to know if I was clean. I felt like a walking disease.

No one would talk to us, let alone see us. Touch? Hell no! I was a loss before I even entered a room. I was thirteen years old. Everywhere I went, I felt like I was trying to make up for the deficit of my fate I felt my whole life afterwards. No matter where I went, I couldn't escape the shame of the disease that killed my father and that somehow I survived.

On the set of *Six Days, Seven Nights*, I was called into Harrison's trailer one lunch break within the first week of shooting and was met with the sight of Ivan and Harrison sitting on one of two white pleather sofas. I hesitantly sat on the opposite white pleather, the tension in the air similar and not unfamiliar, as the air the Four Seasons had been at the press junket for *Volcano*.

   IVAN: Why can't you just be like Jodie Foster?
   ANNE: What does that mean, exactly? (I sort of
      knew it meant they did not want me to be so open
      about my relationship with Ellen.)

They had the news on the television showing the five o'clock report. Apparently, there were rumors that Ellen and I were pregnant. Our "pregnancy" was everywhere. They showed me this as proof of why this openness about my relationship was becoming a pain in the ass for them. Meanwhile, I had no idea. I found it odd that anyone thought I could get pregnant so quickly with a woman, but even odder, that they *cared* so much about the perception that I was, what, exactly? Going to ruin a movie that hadn't even been shot?

The most devastating thing of all, through it all, from the first week with Ellen to writing my first book, was that no one bothered to ask me about *any* of it. There was a complete lack of curiosity. There was a void in the culture that—no matter how many articles were written about me—kept anyone from actually *asking* me to find out why I had done what I did. What was the force that would have made a human being risk everything they'd been promised, their entire career so far, to make a decision that no one else had made so publicly before that time? *Why?* Why would I have done that?

Since nobody asked, I will tell you why. Because I had lived in a family that was built upon lies. My father hid his sexuality his entire life. When I met Ellen and she was open and honest about her sexuality, it was the most attractive and alluring quality in a person that I had ever seen. I was mesmerized by her honesty, and that is why she was the first and only woman that I ever fell in love with.

(I asked again.)
ANNE: What do you mean?
IVAN: Everybody knows it, she just doesn't talk about it.

I couldn't imagine how many things Jodie Foster had chosen not to talk about, but I assumed they were talking specifically about a rumored sexual orientation she had, which she considered no one else's business. And I agreed, then and now—it wasn't.

But I was in a different conundrum: I was in love with a person who had chosen to leverage her very public persona in support of the cause she was standing up for, which was LGBTQ+ rights for everybody on the planet who wanted them. One person's incredible courage— it had nothing to do with anyone else's choices. I felt uniquely called to honor and recognize her courage and join her in her cause.

I wasn't honored by being asked to join Jodie's privacy. I was being asked to deny my choice to stand with Ellen, making our truth and love public.

Let me be clear: Jodie Foster is a hero to me. Her talent, so young, rose above to a pinnacle of fame. She was stalked and her life was threatened daily, and yet she kept pursuing her craft.

Put simply: at that moment, I realized there were two parts to this equation. One is to refuse to lie. The other is to have the confidence, the courage, and the safety to tell the truth. You can't do the first if the conditions aren't there for the second, and love is the fastest way to navigate the truth. To decide to take the risk and know when to speak out. To open yourself to whatever may come.

This math can get complicated by how people react to those reaching for their truth. Sometimes you meet others who truly hate or are afraid of that truth. Who will deny and fight you. Other times, people may support you or say they don't mind (and they really may not, as Harrison and Ivan didn't—they were just reacting to pressure being put on them in turn); but they might trip over their own habits of resistance before standing with you. Everyone must learn to find their own voice. But it's still demeaning to have your truth be reduced to an *inconvenience*, much less a silencing. That's really why, and when, I decided to stay loud.

When I wrote *Call Me Crazy*, my first and only previous book, the odds were against me that it would be a success. At the time my relationship with Ellen had ended; the news was calling me *Ellen-candy*. Publishers only gave me the opportunity to tell my story because of the ruckus we'd caused and the media attention around the breakup. I was a trend that they wanted to take advantage of. They didn't know my voice. They didn't care.

Something was better than nothing. There was an auction for my book, as I recall, that eventually led to a bid so ridiculous, in numbers so big, it would never be paid back. I cost Simon & Schuster hundreds of thousands of dollars that I stashed someplace, knowing it was my safety, my miracle money given by the universe. It was money that would allow me to have a child: the only thing I ever thought was my calling in life. I needed to know what it felt like to have a child in my arms and give to it what I had never been given. It seemed so simple, looking back at my childhood, which so lacked it, to give love.

Love became my destiny and my purpose. I risked everything for it—I still will. Nothing will ever take away from my yearning to discover deeper love. It has its challenges and its rewards, none of which are unimportant.

I wrote *Call Me Crazy* in an ancient villa, on the hill of an actual, for-real castle in Tuscany that I found on the Internet after having a dream telling me to write in Italy. Coincidently, this was during pilot season. People were hesitant to hire me because of my "gay tendencies" and irrational behavior and other various issues. I packed my bag in the middle of winter and flew away to write a book, because a higher power was calling me to do it. And for some odd reason, I always heeded the call. Come agent or manager, logic or reason, I had privately agreed to listen to my higher power, the God I knew. The voice within that encouraged me to follow my intuition and take dares.

If I had known what I do now, I may not have done it. I told everyone to fuck off, ignored countless wisdoms, accepted a free-spirited lover as a traveling companion (my true believer at the time, and not coincidentally, the father of my firstborn), got on a flight, and took off to nowhere I'd ever been. I had never written a book. I had read less than I had written. I was raised on the Bible and made my living playing twins on television. I was so deep into the unknown that my lover Coley had to educate me. Upon the first night's reading of my day's work, standing in front of a fireplace so tall it could have eaten us both, handing the pages I read out loud to my patient and encouraging mate, I was schooled on paragraphs and the purpose of an "indent."

ANNE: Indent. Yes. Absolutely. You got it. What's an indent?

I will always admire Coley for his response to me that night, as we read the pages so much was riding on. I was afraid for my future and nervous about revealing my soul on the page, right there in black and white.

COLEY: You know what? Forget about it. It's not important. Write your way—the rules can be figured out later.

Six weeks later, after countless overseas faxes of completely raw material, the publisher, Lisa Drew, told me she wanted to release my book a great deal earlier than expected. There had been talk about ghostwriters as the first fax arrived, unexpected and without indents. No one really believed I could actually write the book myself. Yet—here was this accomplished editor and expert, saying she would publish my book, word for word—but one.

LISA DREW: I think in the third paragraph, middle sentence, the word *prescient* would be more suitable.
(I didn't know what that word meant. I hated my ignorance. She didn't judge me.)

ANNE: No one will believe me if I write that word.

(I felt like I wasn't smart enough to compete. Not going to college had come to bite me in the ass.)

LISA: You always knew what was coming—you saw what no one else could.

ANNE: That's what that word means? "Prescient." I see the future—I always have.

LISA: (chuckling) You can be stubborn and learn along the way. We're here to help.

I changed the word and accepted the challenge of embracing the next level. It included indents and syllables and acceptance of myself for seeing what no one else was meant to see, except me, maybe. Making choices for yourself, for your life, sometimes doesn't include others. It may alienate and anger. It may be a bust. But if your life depends on it, if the God inside you calls you to action, I bet it's for a good reason.

Life is for you to decide, even if think you don't matter. What is right for you is right for no other; they may not or cannot understand, so don't waste your time asking them to.

Be supportive of others the way you would like to be supported. Encourage greatness so that we all may partake in the glory and wisdom of others. Risk everything you know to be taught, and even what you don't know. Trust the prescience in and of your consciousness that guides you to dive safely into the unknown future of your most magnificent self.

The world is better with more of us participating in goodness for others: in offering kindness without restraint. In risking confusion for clarity. In asking more of ourselves than we ask of others. In doing what we believe is right, even with no support. And demanding that we never falter in the truth: that being here together on this Earth *is* the blessing. We are more together. There is no need for war with each other. More people is more love. God is more. God is you. Offer it, you'll see.

PRACTICE: FACING YOUR FEARS

Nobody ever told me that fears are a learning experience. It makes sense; the family I was raised in were the ones creating my fears. I think a lot of us have had the same experience. We had no safety. There wasn't an atmosphere of feeling good from the time we awoke in the morning to the time we went to bed each night. Each of us has a different story, yet so many of us are connected by the confusion of why we didn't feel good. As a young person, you have no explanation of why you feel unsafe or how you might try to change that; you simply know that you feel it. There was no information or guidance or communication about what we could do about it. The prevalence of this reality for so many has become the curiosity of my life, the study of it, and the commitment. I have always been interested in the *why* of the void of joy in the daily experience of so many people.

I believe it is our right to have a joyous experience from the moment we are birthed onto this planet to the moment we leave it. I have observed many obstacles along that path. I have sympathy and compassion for the generations of conditioning that have led us to the place that has made that right secondary to the fight for control. The lack of understanding is another obstacle, as we have not been offered enough consistent knowledge to choose something else. That time must come to an end.

Discovering the definition of what love means to you and *you alone* is the key to expanding your consciousness. Serving love daily without exception and no intervention from others connects the heart to the mind. The heart and mind connection activates the body to interact with consciousness.

Once your heart and mind are connected with your body, as an adult, it is possible to look back on your past self with compassion for that confusion and bring the knowledge won through hard-earned experience to bear on your present-day life. Give yourself the kindness and love you would give to anyone else in your position. Some of your fears are justified. Some of them are your brain's way of protecting you from situations where you have been hurt in the past, but they may not be useful anymore in your current moment. Consider your fears. Examine them. It's frightening and uncomfortable, but only you can take what you need from your fears.

What is useful? What have you learned? Are there things you would do differently now in similar situations, that your fear has taught you? Are there things that aren't useful? Has your past experience made you afraid in ways that no longer help you, if they ever did? Assess what you have learned. Some of it you will want to take with you, and some of it you will want to discard. Clear your mind of what's no longer useful, so that you aren't carrying baggage that you don't need and that will only weigh you down. The extra mental and emotional space you give yourself leaves more room for the practice of joy.

CHALLENGE: SEE THE TRUTH AROUND YOU

The light of the universe connects you to the world around you and your life. The choices you make are influenced by your past and by the things around you, so let yourself listen to yourself. When you look, listen, and learn about your own self, you are more attuned to the universe around you, and you can start to see patterns everywhere you look. Your brain is optimized to recognize patterns, so pay attention to it. Sometimes your subconscious is telling you something your conscious self hasn't yet acknowledged.

Let yourself be open to the patterns and listen to your gut. Then, as you go about your day, look and listen for signs that confirm your intuition. It can be something as simple as a song coming on the radio or your playlist that seems to align with your gut feeling, or seeing something unusual in nature that seems to align with your decision or thoughts. You are part of the universe, and the universe is part of you, so open yourself up to its messages. Think about tracing your life events and the important people who have come into your life. You might be surprised that the thread began when you were most open to the universe. Consider that you actually didn't have much to do with creating these moments—it's not as if you could decide "today, I'm going to encounter the person who will give me my next job." It's more that you were there to receive them, when something just felt right, or called your attention.

Sometimes the patterns you see are your own gut intuition telling you that you've made a good choice, or that you're not sure about a course of action, so try to listen. Tune into that sense of things clicking into place—or the times when your intuition tells you things are definitely *not* working—and incorporate that awareness into your actions. Trust yourself. This is how we can make bold decisions with confidence, knowing that we have our role to play in something bigger than ourselves, so that we may behave in our own, and others', best interests.

CHAPTER NINE

Speak

LESSON: ABUSE MATTERS, AND SO DOES HOW YOU TALK ABOUT IT

I have some regrets, but they're mostly of a violent nature. I regret not kicking Harvey Weinstein in the balls after he opened his hotel room robe to share his dick with me, as an offering: a present! For me? No, you shouldn't have. You *really* shouldn't have. I was as disgusted with his face as I was with him exposing himself to me.

He said, sleazily: "Suck this, and you'll get the job."

Did he really think he'd get away with this? He preyed on the weakest, most fragile group in Hollywood: the want-to-be-starlets who mostly come from nothing or very little. A good percentage are poor—or will be if they don't get a job soon! Isolated in a town they likely traveled miles and many heartbreaks to get to, lucky enough to win an audition of any kind, let alone with the top movie producer in the world at the time—these girls, this talented group of delicate fighters, these innocents are who Harvey fucking Weinstein chose to denigrate while, at the same time, offering to make their dreams a reality. A life built on a lie. He took advantage of his power and position to manipulate them into doing what they would never have chosen to do.

(I know this pattern.)

He wouldn't have the nerve to hit on a woman. I will tell, tell it from a mountaintop! No one who sees Harvey's dick chooses to suck it or fuck it willingly. I promise you that.

Around the same time as the incident with Harvey Weinstein, in the early 90's, I was also being sexually harassed by the late director, Donald Cammell, on his film, *Wild Side*. It was one of the worst movies ever made—possibly *the* worst movie ever made. (Except I got to work with Christopher Walken and Joan Chen, which was a huge check in the pro column as I tried to weigh whether I should quit the film.) The truth is, when I decided to try to quit, the bosses threatened to sue me.

I was maybe twenty-four years old. And a movie studio was going to sue *me*? It certainly didn't make financial sense. I felt they meant they'd try to ruin me, by taking my dignity and telling the acting community that I was uncooperative on set, all because I wouldn't finger Donald's wife in his office, a necessary step, according to him, to test if I could pull off a convincing lesbian sex scene with the gorgeous Joan Chen. China, Donald's wife, was apparently very comfortable with her sexuality, and he said she could help *me* get comfortable with *mine*.

I said, "I think I got this, thanks, Donald. How about I act like I know what I'm doing?" *Just like I do everything else in my life.*

Aside from how questionable and uncomfortable the entire scenario was, I found the whole notion of someone else getting *me* comfortable with my own sexuality to be completely beside the point. What's so different about filming a sex scene with a man or a woman? What's so different about having sex with a man or a woman? What are people so concerned about? You think seeing a vagina for the first time is any less or more confusing than seeing a dick?

It took twenty years for me to see enough and learn enough to be able to assess the dangers in psychological destitution and create something else as an option. Getting to the other side of the "disease"—the aftermath of trauma and abuse—is an agreement you make with yourself. It's an action that deserves a practice that is supported by others.

I hope the world is learning that we must commit to zero tolerance for abuse. There is no such thing as a little abuse. There's no excuse for it. None is okay. Period. Zero. It shouldn't be a debate whatsoever. No one should ever have to experience what I did.

I'm fifty-three years old as of this writing. I've survived countless horrors. I've seen my siblings die. I've survived abuse and homelessness and grew up amid a criminal cover-up of a cult that buried children before allowing them to speak the truth of what they witnessed. I was sexually harassed, and my livelihood—my reputation and sense of worth—threatened if I did not comply. And through all of it I was expected to keep silent.

I was born into a sex cult. I was physically, mentally, and verbally raped of my identity from the time I was a child, and now I have found my way to sanity and have the privilege to share what I've learned. I've come to understand that I have been a participant in a disease that has spread worldwide: abuse. Abuse does not come in one form or from one congregation. It is not taught as a reality nor preached as religion. It is an insidious, agreed-upon, dark layer of the universal consciousness that has debilitated our communities, our religions, our politics, our cultures, our leadership, our families, our educational systems, our friendships, our homes, and our lifestyles. Abuse is the lie that permeates the reality that we are living in and has become an accepted foundation of our everyday life. We live in a lie, and it is time for it to be called out and ended once and for all.

We abide in a culture built on and living in the acceptance of hatred and abuse. We accept agreements passed through generations that we have stopped questioning and blindly absorb. We believe that one is not equal to another. We think *I am* and *they are not*. We war and we fight and we divide and we conquer one over another. This culture of domination is expressed through control, manipulation, and overpowering people who don't have the means or power to resist.

The culture of abuse is about hiding and terror. My childhood memories include being locked in dark places, met with masked men and women in shadow so as to not be able to identify the abusers. You are only allowed to be seen in the light of the places the abusers choose, so that they may control the situation. In church, of course, the congregation is all under their insidious control, so all eyes are the punisher. In school, you are sent to corners during recess and lunch to read your pocket Bible and memorize that week's verses. No talking, no sharing. Separation from the group is completely forbidden for fear anyone should be exposed to the secrets held within the cult's systematic brainwashing.

The culture of abuse empowers the abusers and silences their victims. Only together do we have the ability to resist. Only when those girls that Harvey abused came together to speak their truths did anything change.

We are stronger together. If we can extend acceptance to each other and break the secrecy and shame imposed on us from the outside, then can we begin to heal.

You don't have to go to the newspapers, but it is healing to speak the truth of what an abuser has done, if only to yourself. Say it out loud. Say it alone, if that feels better to you, but know that if you speak your truth to others, you will find that there are other people who have experienced similar things—far too many of them.

We can embrace our differences. I will never be you, and you may not want to be me. But focusing on those differences is a distraction and can be an excuse not to take action. Our similarities are greater. Together we are stronger. Together we are *more*. We are better together.

PRACTICE: HEALING

Admitting that you have been sexually abused in this society is dismissed as easily as if you had claimed that God himself had raped you. To tell or not to tell: this is the devastating question and the constant conundrum of an abused child. The fear of disbelief looms large.

The first step is to ask ourselves if we want to change that reality. The second step is to understand that we can. And the third step is to embrace the truth that with our participation we have the power to eradicate abuse for ourselves and forever.

There are difficult, hellish truths, and they exist on this planet worldwide in more incarnations than we care to face. The abuse I endured is only one facet of the suffering people inflict on each other. It is destruction of the soul, and it is a disease. I would rather die than not expose the truth I know.

The way to begin healing from that kind of abuse is to bring it into the light. The truth of what you endure is the way to be free of it. My abusers thrived in an environment of secrets and shame.

I have no special gift. I was born into a world of deep sorrow and the acceptance of its denial. I was brought to the ground, nearly tortured to death so that I would not speak what I knew and what I saw. But I was too young and too uneducated and too damn stubborn not to escape it. My ignorance was my blessing, and being ignored was my pathway out.

I was taught the message of Jesus Christ. By being fed the verses in the Bible day after day, I was able to access the difference between the message I was learning and the actions and behavior the people around me exhibited. The miracle of my life is that I was able to differentiate between a language that was being called love and the reality of being treated with hate.

Three of my siblings are dead. My father died of AIDS. These are facts. Hiding is not what I'm interested in. I never have been. I'm here to tell my truth and offer an option to the culture of hate dominating our societies and poisoning our children. I can't do anything about what has been, but I can offer an option of what could be. Simply put: love.

I was born into a box. We are all in some way or another. I will never be the queen of England or the emperor of Japan. As an actor, you often hear yourself compared to other people, and it's important to understand and accept that those comparisons are unnecessary. I won't be anyone else. They will never be *me*. This acceptance is the beginning of peaceful living. We are born without choice of who we are and the circumstances we come into, but we can choose how we go on once we are grown. The greatest equation we are challenged to solve is how to own our own experience and learn how to choose what to do with the life offered ahead of us.

Choice is the greatest power we have. We wake, we see, we feel, we decide, we act, we interact, we work, we play, we create, we experience, each and every day. It is ours to decide and take control of what that looks like, what that feels like, and how we make others interact with our choices.

CHALLENGE: TELL THE TRUTH

Speak truth.

Though the world can be full of pain and difficulty, pain and shame are perpetuated by secrecy. People will tell you that your truths aren't true. People often believe abusers over the people they hurt. Perhaps it's because they don't want to believe what cruelty people are capable of; perhaps it's because they want to be absolved of the pain that happened to others. But even if the only one witnessing your difficulties is you, your truths and your suffering are important.

You can and should speak your truths, if only to yourself. You know best what is happening to you and what you have gone through.

I feel most connected to my thoughts when I write longhand. You might find it useful to type into a document or put down your thoughts on index cards. I love writing in a beautiful journal, but some people feel almost paralyzed by the pressure to write something meaningful in a "fancy" journal or notebook. If that's you, grab a spiral-bound notebook, or a composition book like you used to use in school, and a ballpoint pen. The vessel you're writing in isn't as important as your thoughts, so experiment and find what you're most comfortable with.

Likewise, different times of day might work better for you. Some people find it's easiest to connect with the deeper level of their mind if they write in the morning, right after they wake up, before their brain has had a chance to get cluttered with thoughts about what they have to do that day. Alternatively, some people find it's easiest to write just before bedtime, when they can sort through and catalog the events of the day. The important thing is to get your thoughts on paper.

Keep a journal for a period of time. Give yourself a month to play around with when and where you write. It doesn't have to be a long entry. I find a good way to get started is to set a timer—say, for ten minutes to start; you can always go longer if you feel like it—and don't stop writing the entire time. You can set yourself a prompt. What do you hope for in the day ahead? What went right or wrong about the day you just had? Choose a time in your life, past, present, or future, and write about it. If there's a thorny problem you're wrestling with, or a memory troubling you, take the time to write down what bothers you about it and how you feel about it. Or if that's too heavy, focus on what you're grateful for or a kindness someone has shown you. Sometimes bringing your attention to what's good about *today* can be enough to shift your entire mood into the light.

Here's a list of sample prompts that I have used to help get to know myself better:

- Envision an imaginary door that leads to *more* in your life. What is holding it shut? What is the key to unlock it? What are the ways I can give myself permission to step through the door?

- I am responsible for finding my own way and forging my own path. What are my goals? What can I do for myself to help myself reach them?

- What are the reasons I want to explore *more*? How can I prepare to be surprised by what the universe brings me? How can I make a space for myself that's mine and *only* mine?

- Am I able to close the door on things in my past? How can I give myself grace for mistakes I've made and let go of emotions that weigh me down so I can move forward into joy?

These are simply ways to open your mind to your own goals and emotions. Try to come up with your own list of prompts to set for yourself. You know best the topics that are most important to you. Give yourself the gift of time spent setting down your thoughts about those topics. You will find that knowing yourself better than you did before is its own reward. Rather than assigning blame or judgment, work on your relationship with *yourself*. Honesty is key; if you can't tell the truth to yourself, then who can you tell it to?

CHAPTER TEN

Create

LESSON: THE WOW GENERATION

The smallest gestures can have the most magnificent impact. Every time I leave town for a job, I get a little depressed. It has never been easy for me to leave my sons. Even though I feel all the logic and reason and excitement and purpose: I need to get a paycheck just like we all do. I'm proud of how I am able to get mine. I'm proud of what I do. I'm honored to be asked to perform for a living, with all the amazing artists I get the chance to work with. All the things you may imagine life as a movie actor entails, if you have ever cared to imagine it. Believe me, I am not assuming you think about my life on set! You have your own lives to think about. It is a dream, and truly extraordinary, I admit it. And I never forget it—not ever do I take my blessings for granted.

The night of the *Volcano* premiere, in the middle of the third act of the movie, an usher tapped my shoulder and then Ellen's, and without our knowledge as to why, we were ushered out of the theater, pushed into our limo, and sent home.

There would be no pictures at the afterparty of Ellen and me together. There would be no celebration. My date and I were shut down and shut out of the crowd. During this time, there were rumors Ellen was starting to hear that, as spectacular as her coming-out show was, the continuation of *Ellen* was "under consideration." That meant one thing: Ellen was going to be canceled. My three-picture deal with Fox had already been canceled. Together, it seemed like we were an epic fail, at least in terms of our work lives. Within a week after our meeting, we had tanked both our careers and fired everyone who could help.

Had we slept at all, the phone that rang would have jolted us awake. We were in the kitchen—back when people still had kitchen phones—trying to see what could be salvaged of our careers. We both stared at the phone, daring the other to pick up. There had been no *good* news. Ellen was watching the television reports. Hollywood news reports had determined with no hesitation that our mutual decision made in that week was not only detrimental to our careers, but *proof* as to why it was necessary and important for everyone to *stay in the closet*. How dare we try to be open and public about our relationship! Look at what happens to people of the same sex pronouncing love for each other. Both of us were being written off as bad bets, just for wanting to love one another.

This was what Ellen, what my father, what so *many* others have faced, when confronted with the obscure dimension of misunderstanding acting as hatred.

Discrimination was really pissing me off!

(The phone rang again. I picked it up.)
ANNE: Hello?
HARRISON: Can I please speak to Anne?
ANNE: This is she.
HARRISON: This is Harrison.
ANNE: *Ford?*
(I looked at Ellen like, WTF?)
HARRISON: Do you know another Harrison?
ANNE: Well . . . no.
(The next sentence I heard will blow your mind . . .)
HARRISON: Frankly, my dear . . . I don't give a damn who you're sleeping with. We have a job to do together. Let's make the best romantic comedy anybody's ever seen.
ANNE: Are you fucking with me?
HARRISON: Do I sound like I'm fucking with you?
ANNE: (Considers) No.
HARRISON: You didn't fuck with me, so I won't fuck with you.

I still don't know exactly why he chose to help me when it seemed like the entire film industry had decided I was box-office poison. But at the moment my career seemed to be at its lowest, and everything I had worked for was slipping out of my grasp, Harrison reached out and threw me a lifeline. He did me the courtesy of not caring who I was sleeping with. It did—and does—mean the world.

Put simply: Harrison Ford rejected intolerance. He lent his voice to what "Wow" means to me—being accepted for who you are and what you can do, and returning that in kind, even when no one is listening; even when you don't have to. That's the world I'm interested in creating. And just maybe, we're getting closer to "Wow" now than we've ever been.

I'm grateful for all these experiences because they led me to choose love. I've made love my craft, my science, my obsession . . . my purpose. Whatever you want to call it, I served it. I looked for the answers as to why, when we don't understand something, we try and bury it. Even love! If it's expressed in a way people don't immediately grasp—like my falling in love with both a woman and men, at different times—they want to turn what they don't understand into an other they can hate and deride. Why? And I wanted to know how could I help prevent that?

Here's the answer: your side isn't any more valid than their side.

The equation is the simplest and most difficult you will ever face. It's simple math: what you give, you must give unto yourself firstly, so that you access the capability to give to another wholly. There is *no* skipping of the steps. Not because the desire to save another isn't worthy, but because it's impossible. There's a reason they tell you to put your own oxygen mask on first when you get on a plane: you can't help anyone else until you help yourself. Only once you have worked on yourself are you capable of helping anyone else. And even then, you can't do it for them. Just like you, they have to walk their own path.

At the time I was called to the service of love first and given the platform, there was zero language to help us understand the idea of choice in love. Choice didn't come into it! True freedom with our sexuality outside gender was not anything that had been presented as an option before in media and the broader social consciousness. We as a society were just not ready for that way of thinking yet. Believe me, my role in that evolution wasn't intentional. I could not have constructed a path to representing that freedom if I had wanted to. But times are changing, and catching up with love. This generation, beyond any other, knows that there are more ways to be, to explore. More ways to love.

I believe that love has no gender. I believe that we keep ourselves out of the doors that allow us to see the magic. The challenges are the things presented to us where we can block ourselves from understanding because our righteousness gets in the way. We can prevail over any darkness and burst through to the next floor: the door to *more*!

Consciousness is all possibility. If you believe that and want to seek it further, you can begin with discarding

QUESTIONS FOR TRAVELERS

Who am I?
What am I doing here?
Where do I belong?
Where do I go, if I don't know?
How do I find out? Why do I care?
Will it matter? How will I fare?

PRACTICE: HOPE

Hope is more valuable to our happiness than you may think. Hope keeps us motivated when things become difficult and when we have obstacles and roadblocks. It's essential to retain hope when life throws you curveballs. I have a saying that has remained true to me my entire life—"the mistake is the messenger." Meaning that when things go wrong, I firmly believe it is for a reason that eventually reveals itself. It may not seem that way at the time, but that canceled project often opened the door to something better. So the next time something does not go as planned, or you are disappointed, pay attention to the message in the mistake—there's a lesson and inner growth somewhere in your circumstances, even if you don't see it yet. Reflect your hope into the universe, which will give back what you hoped. Visualize the future that you want for yourself and remain optimistic. You might be surprised to know the power you have within yourself.

If we exist in a void of hope, it might be because we haven't agreed on what we want. We have to know what we are hoping for. Only then can we ignite action that connects ourselves to more. Like love, hope begins with a singular commitment with ourselves about who and what we serve. I call this conundrum:

Am I about myself, or am I about others?

Once this decision is made, it becomes the filter for every decision we make. It determines each step we take—every interaction, choice, thought, process, relationship determination, and deposit of ourselves into this universal consciousness.

It isn't easy to open yourself up to hope, especially if you have a history of difficult times in your past. Each time we get hurt, we want to build up our defenses more strongly to protect ourselves. But it would be a mistake to stop hoping. Just because there is a history of pain, we shouldn't cut ourselves off from joy.

It's all too easy to close ourselves off, in expectation for the next painful blow to fall, but instead, try to look for the good things the universe can bring you. Sometimes you might have to look hard! But the act of trying will also nurture hope.

There are times when it feels as though life is nothing but hardships, one trying time after another, with the next challenge coming upon you before you even have time to recover from the one before. But don't only think about the negative consequences of wherever you are; let yourself envision an easier, brighter time ahead of you. You can plan for the worst but hope for the best. Sometimes that means looking for whatever kernels of good you can find in what seems like nothing but a bad situation. Sometimes you're forced to leave your community and move somewhere new, but that experience gets you to a school where the teachers are there to nurture your gifts, where chance and a snowstorm bring opportunity into your life, and where you find a new career that will change your life. Leave yourself open to possibilities, no matter how far-fetched they might seem, and let yourself hope.

EXACTNESS

Love is a practice.
It is an art.
Love is a seeking
Love is the start.

Mistakes are teachers
Learning a must
Detours God's actions
That lead us to trust.

Common is yesterday
Lazy is stubborn
Life offers choices
Risk is forlorn.

All knowing is farce
No one is all
That's where we depart
Diverge from the call.

It's ours to wonder
The spirit of quest
I offer a ponder,
The door that opens "Yes."

CHALLENGE: STATE YOUR PLEASURE

Why is sex so fun to talk about? *Except* with certain lovers? Is this familiar to anyone . . .

> YOU: You're perfect. Everything you did and *do* is perfect! It . . . (You have no words!)
> (As you are running to the bathroom to wash *it* off.)
> THEM: Are you sure? Was I too fast?
> YOU: No! Honey! It was perfect. *All of it.*
> (We know what to say because we say it every time.)
> THEM: I wasn't too fast?
> YOU: Fast . . . ha! Perfect, more like! Your size is perfect, your style is perfect, that was amazing! . . . Almost.

They're so psyched at this point by their "good performance." They then return to their phone screens, satisfied that they tapped that shit *good*.

But did they? Or did they forget that one of the words in the comment that made them feel so good about themselves and their prowess as a lover was *almost*? So often, we don't say anything. We are back to feeling bad about ourselves and wondering why we did not tell the truth that it was not actually good for us. We quickly determine that we will not have bad sex again. And we don't—until the next time.

So your nonorgasmic nights get drowned in self-loathing, which is where most women feel more comfortable than addressing the topic of the *vagina* and how to make it feel good. You turn your internal monologue onto your partner's flaws as well as your own, and once you get going, you can get a list that ranges from their stupid haircut to the way they forgot your birthday to the fact that their favorite food is hard-boiled eggs *and* the fact that they crack the shells wrong! You can forget why you were attracted to and cared about them in the first place—and you forget that for anything to actually change, you have to talk about it first. As much as you might want your partner to read your mind, the only way they can do that is if you tell them what you're thinking.

Oftentimes, resentment builds up when there's a change you want but you haven't had the courage to make it happen. It might get to the point where it explodes out of you. You might end up insulting them every way you can think of, and while some of your complaints may have merit, the only change that's going to result out of that is one or both of you ending the relationship.

So if you want to actually make a change that doesn't completely finish off any chance of turning that *almost* into an *oh yes*, you need to buckle down and communicate. It can be frightening and uncomfortable to let someone know that what they're doing in the bedroom isn't working for you, but it's like every other area of life—the truth, along with kindness and love will bring you joy. It's hard for you to talk about, try showing them. The only thing you have to lose is a bad time in bed, and what you gain is trust and joy.

Remember: bottling it up only leads to drama and dissatisfaction. You can deepen trust by saying what you want. Honesty can lead to joy!

CHAPTER ELEVEN

Live

THE PRACTICE OF JOY

The disease of abuse has followed me my entire life. Acting was my ticket out of a home that never felt safe or comfortable for me, and I never could have predicted the places it would take me or the people I would meet. I could never have predicted that I would meet and love a woman, or that I would become known as one of the faces of gay rights in the media. But through all the high points of my career and the struggles of my private life I have come to understand and believe in a philosophy that looks for the good and the beautiful in everyone, as well as embraces those who are struggling.

If there is one thing I could say to everyone trying to get through their own difficulties, whether the trauma of abuse, or the heartbreak of grief, or the struggle of feeling alone—whatever haunts you, know this: you don't have to prove yourself worthy. You matter. There is love and beauty inside you, and it connects you to a wide, wonderful universe. There is light all around us, and it connects us.

Put simply: we are all part of a greater whole, and not one of us is more important than any other. You, me—every single human being out there—we are all part of something bigger than us, the *more* that makes us part of the living, breathing universe.

The philosophy that I have developed over my life and put into action is the practice of joy. The things that bring the most light into the world are love, truth, and kindness, and so I have tried to live my life with these values as my signposts. These are concepts that can be put into action, and if you are consistent with these actions, you will find your own practice of joy. It's my hope that the challenges and prompts in this book have encouraged you to open your heart and your mind to the joy that surrounds you, even and *especially* if your life is difficult. There's beauty and love to be found even in the midst of whatever pain your life holds. Keep love in your heart and curiosity and a willingness to learn in your mind, and your practice will sustain you. That's the purpose of the practice.

Forgiveness is essential when you make mistakes. Mistakes are inevitable. We are all human, and that means we are both glorious and flawed. It's important to be able to forgive yourself when you mess up. Everyone makes mistakes out of ignorance sometimes. You don't always know what you're doing, or that something you said or did might have inadvertently hurt someone. The important thing to do is give yourself grace. Take what you learn from that experience, and you can resolve not to make exactly the same mistake again. It's far too easy to say something hurtful without meaning to—like telling an entire march of LGBTQ+ people that their sexuality is a choice. But once you learn why what you said or did is harmful, you have the choice of doubling down and insisting you are right no matter what anyone tells you—or listening to what other people say and considering their point of view. They are just as important as you, and you are just as important as them, so you can choose to have respect for the humanity of those around you and to look for people who give you that respect in return.

Sometimes you might act in a way that is not in alignment with your values, and not from a place of you being your best self. It's okay; grant yourself grace here, too. People act out of anger or sadness or negativity sometimes, in ways they might later regret. Perhaps you are one of them. Have compassion for your previous self as well as the people you hurt. It's not always possible to make amends, but you can learn from that experience and resolve to do better going forward. If you find there's a pattern in your life of lashing out in anger or reacting in ways that feel out of your control, try and analyze your reactions and look for causes and effects. This is another great topic to take into your journal or diary so you can really think about why you behave the way you behave.

Once you see a pattern, you can choose to break it. If you know there's a topic or situation that gets you to a place where your emotions run high and you don't feel in control, think about how you can redirect those emotions when they come up. Maybe it's as simple as avoiding that person or situation. Perhaps you need to practice drawing a boundary—if your coworker or mother-in-law thinks your allergies are made up, for example, practice changing the topic to something completely different if they try to steer the conversation that way—and perhaps don't eat any food they offer you. If you and your partner always fight about whose turn it is to do the dishes, or who forgot whose birthday, practice taking a time-out. You could say something like, "I'm too upset to talk about this right now. Let's talk about it in the morning when my emotions aren't so high." (Pro tip: you can say this even when you think it's the *other* person's emotions that are running high. They might want to argue that they're not really that upset in that moment, but they can't tell you how you feel.) Then, at a calmer time, you can readdress the topic at hand and try to come up with solutions together. If they keep trying to talk about it when you've called a time-out, remove yourself from the situation. You can go to another room or leave the house for a little while. You don't have to engage when you've decided you're not in the right frame of mind to talk about it.

These strategies are intended to help you tell your truth. Honesty will help free you from the pain that secrecy and shame can bind you in.

Our life is full of doors, open and closed. I don't mean the doors in your house, although of course those exist, too—I mean the doors in your head. When you open a door in your *mind*, you get access to another floor of your consciousness, and you take one step farther into the more that is being connected with the universe. Some of the doors are already open. Some, you don't even know that they're closed. You might not even know that they exist! But as you dig deeper into your own thoughts and values, and as you open yourself up to love and the truth around you, more doors open. Sometimes the door might stay closed because opening it seems frightening, or too difficult to contemplate. But the key to opening it is within you—you just have to look and find your own superpowers.

Sometimes we have wounds from our past that make opening these doors more difficult. It's natural to want to favor the injured or bruised places in your mind and soul the way you would a physical energy, but unless you address the issue, you might end up limping. Treat yourself gently, but really think about why those places hurt. Sometimes it's obvious—if you slipped and fell down a flight of stairs, one reaction might be to avoid staircases altogether. You're so afraid you might fall and reinjure yourself that you don't ever want to take the steps again. Another reaction might be to recklessly run down every set of steps you see, trying to prove to yourself that you're not afraid of the stairs, even after what happened to you. Even if that might be setting yourself up to get hurt again! Or another reaction might be to take care of the injury and still take the steps but proceed with caution and hold on to the safety rail. None of those reactions are *wrong*, but you have to be aware of whether or not they are truly working for you. There is no point in judging yourself for your reaction; instead, simply take note of it as an information point. Once you have the information, then you can address whether that reaction is useful to your life going forward. Maybe you are happy with how you approach the steps after falling down them, and nothing needs to change. But if your approach isn't working for you, then once you've thought about it and analyzed it, you can make changes if you need to and open a new door. Once you've gotten to know yourself a little bit better, it's that much easier to find the key.

Creativity can unlock your boundless potential. I hope that the challenges in this book can be a starting point for you to find your own methods of connecting yourself to the universe so you can feel yourself to be part of a greater whole. Speaking truth, making a practice of kindness, and embracing the love within yourself and that the world gives to you are your pieces to the puzzle of creating your own practice of joy. The methods in this book are a vital jumping-off point, but only you can determine the shape your own practice will take.

Keep your focus on what's important to you. If you find yourself feeling dull to the world around you, try to engage with your creativity to wake yourself up.

Don't let yourself sleepwalk through your life—not when you have the opportunity to be awake and aware to the possibilities around you and to prioritize your development in your own spirituality. Allow yourself the benefits of being kind as a purposeful everyday practice. I do not belong to any organized religion, but I have tried to make the intentional practice of kindness in action my religion. If you give it a try, you will find that it can make an enormous difference in your life.

Trauma may have informed your life, but you can make your own path. The only person who can do that work is you, but it is such worthwhile work. I hope the tools in this book help shape your path, help you find your own truths to get a better idea of who you are as a person, and help move you through whatever challenges—past, present, or future—you might find yourself facing.

No matter what pain you've experienced or hardships you've endured, and no matter what anyone else has said about you or to you, I want you to remember that you are worthy, and you are important, and you—yes, you!—have the ability, the means, and the strength to shape your own life.

Go forth with the tools and the knowledge you have gained and use them to craft your own intentionally joyful life. With all the kindness, love, joy, and truth in your soul, you can make yourself a better, more honest, happier life. I hope this book has gotten you started and that what you have learned here can help you make a future full of connection and purpose.

Remember: Anne says you can do it! You have the power within. Believe in your soul that you are indestructible.

GIVE IS THE KEY

ove is at the very heart of my philosophy, and the center of the practice of joy. When things are difficult, it's all too easy to fold up into ourselves and isolate ourselves from the world around us. It's understandable; it's a protective instinct. You curl up into a little ball to hide your vulnerable underbelly and raise your hard shell around yourself because it feels safer that way. But you are also cutting yourself off from the feelings and experiences that bring meaning to life. I believe in love. I believe in kindness. I believe in joy. These are the central tenets of how I live my life, and what I most want you to take away from this book. They are simple concepts, but they are not always easy to put into practice.

How can you put them into practice in your own life? I hope that the challenges and thought exercises in this book have sparked ideas about ways to be kinder and more loving to yourself and those around you, but for this challenge, I want you to think about what you can give to the people you love in your own life, and to your community.

There are a lot of reasons for this. The most important is that it's a way to bring the love that's inside you out to the wider world. The things you can give of yourself on a daily basis don't have to be dramatic gestures. You're not out to change the whole world, but to increase the levels of love and kindness in the world drop by drop. Over time, these actions wear away the coldness, hate, and indifference around us as surely as water slowly wearing away stone.

So what does giving of yourself to the world around you look like? It's going to vary from person to person. What you choose to do should be meaningful to you, because the more it means to you, and the more you enjoy it, the more likely you are to keep doing it—and that way you brought joy to yourself as well as the person you're giving to.

As well, you can start small. Perhaps one day your giving might look like deciding to pick up coffee for a coworker or a friend, and another day, it might look like paying for the person behind you in the Starbucks drive-through. Maybe it's a kind word to a stranger you're passing by who you'll never meet again. You might want to volunteer your time to activities that increase levels of positive energy in the world. You can think about things that are meaningful to you. Sometimes it's obvious. Maybe your grandfather lost his vision, so you might volunteer to read stories for the vision impaired, either through your local library or an online resource like ReadThisToMe.org. Or perhaps the last several years have brought your attention to community food banks, and you donate to the one in your community. Or maybe you just make a batch of sandwiches to give to anyone you see on the streets who is hungry. There are so many areas in which the world could use some help.

Ask yourself what positive things you can put into the universe and commit yourself to making them happen. It can be as simple as extending grace, patience, and compassion to the people around you, and remembering that everyone around you has their own burdens to bear, and a smile or a moment of kindness from a stranger can make a world of difference to someone who's struggling.

And I'll tell you a secret. When things are their most difficult, extending kindness to someone else who needs it, maybe just as much as you do in that moment, can make you feel better. Of course, helping someone else won't make your own problems simply disappear, but at a time when it's most difficult to get outside your own head, doing something for someone else can help put your worries into perspective.

So, choose a way to put kindness and honesty into practice and give to the people around you. You might be surprised by how much joy it brings to you, too.

Anne's 20 Commitments

1. STOP: ignoring what you know
2. RISK: looking further
3. BUILD: a community of zero tolerance
4. BE: a leader that demands full disclosure
5. KNOW: what you see
6. HEAL: with kindness
7. CREATE: purpose within yourself
8. TAKE: yourself out of the equation
9. THINK: of others first
10. LISTEN: to what you hear

11. EXPLORE: possibility
12. BIRTH: compassion for yourself and others
13. CHOOSE: equity always and minorities first
14. USE: your gifts
15. SURPRISE: yourself and others
16. FACE: your fears
17. COMMIT: to offering more
18. ACCEPT: guidance willingly
19. EXPERIMENT: just try it
20. LIVE OUT LOUD: be yourself

JUNIPER SEA

I am a juniper sea greeting the tides of sway,
in my recital of gay restless Wonder of scent and
    flavor and
Color-unrest within tide and ride of splendor
    unknown,
awaiting the collide of bold and fervor that takes
    no
Prisoner but ourselves in the surprising fear that
greets its mate, the thing always wanted in our
    debate
of whether or not we will encourage The Fate upon
    its arrival.

But now, as the time of its happening becomes
    present,
we question its prescience as foolery and seek
    permission
from any other to relieve Us of our birth right's
    pleasure
to choose the "yes" of our quest with not one
    percent doubt,
as the tiniest of "No thanks, too much for me"
is the halt of the glee when entering the door of
Unbounded free that cannot be your experience
if any singular choice, however small, belongs in the
    hands of another.

The worldly-God is funny like that, as there is no
    zero point
to connect, if at all relying on the key of something
    or someone Other.
The pressure of this grandeur is the drive and force
    to awake
Into the spirit of the wholly Grace that replaces fear
    in its wake.

Come holy ocean, scent and taste. A new life meant
    for
you to embrace what's true. Running from the sun
    is what
Society has done to transform us into puppets of
    abuse.

Now is the time to flip the dime, state the old as
    unfun, demand it undone
and arrive at the place of joining God's grace,
each and every one deserving its taste.

I say "No thanks" to the walls that have been built
    around,
through towers of babble and endless mind-scrabble,
deceiving the self by teaching something else.

Goodbye sin, Hello grin, Kick the lie away as of
    this Day.
The day I say I am here to stay and no one or sum
Can convince me any other way.
I'll meet you where the Juniper meets the sea,
and ever more choose to be free.

You + Me = WE

Epilogue

BY HEATHER DUFFY

met Anne in 2010 at the historic Los Angeles Tennis Club. At this same club in 1955, an eleven-year-old Billie Jean King was excluded from a photo for wearing shorts instead of a tennis skirt. In her autobiography, King said, "I think I sensed without ever really being able to say it that if I ever got the chance, I was going to change tennis, if I could, and try to get it away from that kind of nonsense." So, the irony was not lost on me when I first met Anne on the tennis court. She bounded onto a court of housewives awash in Lululemon tennis outfits, wearing sweatpants and a T-shirt, without a racket. For those who don't know, ladies' club tennis can be as intimidating as a boardroom of world leaders. Remembering the first time I walked into this lion's den years before, I felt the need to ease her landing in a way

I wish someone had done for me. I did not know at the time that I would spend the next decade of my life trying to ease her landing. She ultimately became one of my best friends and my business partner, and we cohosted a podcast together. We went through every life event, big or small, as a team for her last decade. Except for this one—her death—which I have to navigate alone.

The end of Anne's story on this earth is immense and tragic, but it does not define her, and it is not the end of Anne. She lives on through her sons and everyone she inspired to seek happiness and show kindness and acceptance to others. Her iconic films will continue to entertain us with her genuinely remarkable talent. Her preparation for each role showed her consideration for every project and everyone working on it. She gave the same respect to the entire crew—from the director to the security guard. Anne had worked since she was twelve years old, and her work ethic was undeniable.

The world is different, having had Anne in it. The impact of her bravery and the sacrifice of standing up for the right to love who you want can be seen on every red carpet today. Anne's public stand for equality empowered many LGBTQ+ people worldwide to see a future where they could live in their truth. I have received so many letters since Anne's passing telling me how being open with her love for another woman gave them the courage to come out to their families, because Anne was someone their parents knew and admired as a celebrity. These messages would have meant the world to her.

Despite being blacklisted and ridiculed, Anne continued to work nonstop after being shut out of studio pictures. She was not offered the prominent roles that would have celebrated her full talent. She was an Emmy winner who did countless films and TV roles. She was nominated for a Tony Award for her role as Lily Garland in *Twentieth Century*. She died with a book coming out, a podcast, five films in postproduction, a recurring TV series role, and several other projects about to begin.

Anne released her first book in September 2001. She flew out of Boston's Logan airport on her way to Toronto the same morning as the terrorists. The book was titled *Call Me Crazy*, and everyone did. But, sadly, they did not see her memoir for the incredible life story of survival that it was. At that time, the world was in shock from September 11, and the only material the late-night pundits had to make fun of was Anne and the title of her book—so they ran with that. So now, in case you did not know the story of why this book is called *Call Me Anne*, please understand that it is an ever-so-gentle, ever-so-slight jab to all those who missed the message on the first go-around. *Call Me Crazy* was Anne's story of triumph: overcoming much to rise to the highest level in an industry that is not easy to break into, and then making a choice of character and integrity that has had a lasting impact on increasing acceptance in our world.

Anne died in the same month that this book was to be finalized for publication, and it represents everything that mattered most to her. There were always more stories to tell, both entertaining and serious, but Anne focused in this book on people and events that helped her shape what she saw as her life's work. Anne's life story is brimming with pain, abuse, and unwarranted judgment, but she never let that define her. Instead, she used it to forge her path, which included honesty, kindness, and joy. Her wish was that this book could help others get to the other side of pain and learn about her philosophy, which allowed her to remain in a life where she woke up each day looking for opportunities to find joy and spread kindness. So, in some ways, knowing her the way I did and knowing that spreading her message of kindness is what mattered to her most, she would be content that the last thing she worked on was this book.

Some might be startled by her stories in this book and the values that guided her life. Her loyal fans will not be surprised, but those of you who did not have the opportunity to look closely at her life and received information peripherally from the media hopefully understand that there is danger in that. Let this book inspire us all to be better, be kinder, look for truth, and avoid basing opinions on speculations or rumors. The media is often a mirror of society, and it's up to us to change what we seek to read. Let's stop looking for negativity and delighting in others' struggles. Maybe we can start to evolve as a society little by little and not find entertainment in the spin of the truth.

In this spirit, I want to acknowledge all of Anne's

fans. We called them fANNEs (Anne always loved a play on words.) So many fANNEs have contacted me with such beautiful words of love and kindness. I've been struck by how often the messages began similarly: *I'm not famous. I'm nobody. I'm just a mom. I am not important.* I need you all to know that you were everything to her. You were her inspiration. Despite spending most of her life in Hollywood, Anne was not impressed or motivated by celebrity. She respected hard work. She was in awe of creativity in spirituality, art, music, and design. She was inspired by those brave and honest enough to embrace their individuality. She thought that kind people were the most beautiful people. Anne was dedicated to her fANNEs. She wrote this book as a thank you and as a guide with the hope that it would give you and others some tools to live a happier life.

Anne's books will continue to tell her story and show generations for years to come that you do not have to be defined by your abuse or by the hand you were dealt. She is proof that even if the world does not always treat you with love and kindness, you have the choice to remain joyful, hopeful, and kind. She never stopped believing this, or trying. It's up to us now to continue her unfinished work.

Anne always talked about the flip side. She even talked about turning this book upside down so you had to flip it to read the second part. She believed that hate was the flip side of love, but it's the one thing she said that I now question. Through Anne's passing, I have